SAP Activate in a Nutshell

By
Sudipta Malakar

FIRST EDITION 2019

Copyright © BPB Publications, INDIA

ISBN: 978-93-88176-87-3

Distributors:

BPB PUBLICATIONS
20, Ansari Road, Darya Ganj
New Delhi-110002
Ph: 23254990/23254991

BPB BOOK CENTRE
376 Old Lajpat Rai Market,
Delhi-110006
Ph: 23861747

MICRO MEDIA
Shop No. 5, Mahendra Chambers,
150 DN Rd. Next to Capital Cinema,
V.T. (C.S.T.) Station, MUMBAI-400 001
Ph: 22078296/22078297

DECCAN AGENCIES
4-3-329, Bank Street,
Hyderabad-500195
Ph: 24756967/24756400

Published by Manish Jain for BPB Publications, 20, Ansari Road, Darya Ganj, New Delhi-110002 and Printed by Repro India Pvt Ltd, Mumbai

Preface

It has been a general observation that most SAP consultants and professionals are used to the conventional waterfall methodology. SAP Activate is an innovative, next generation business suite that allows producing working deliverables straight away.

The traditional Waterfall model has many pitfalls in current market with varying complex customer requirements. SAP Activate Methodology is a harmonized agile implementation approach for cloud, on premise, and hybrid deployments for delivering shippable product increments in an iterative and incremental way. The SAP Activate methodology contains accelerators, tools, templates, questionnaires, checklists, work streams and guidebooks to ensure efficient, consistent, and repeatable delivery of SAP implementations and upgrades. As a successor to traditional implementation methodology, SAP Activate is underused, generally as a little material has been published on the modular and agile framework.

Manage your SAP Project with SAP Activate, will take your learning to the next level. The book promises to make you understand and practice the SAP Activate Framework. The focus is to take you on a journey of all the phases of SAP Activate methodology and make you understand all the phases with real life examples, lessons learnt, accelerators and best practices. Well articulation on how SAP Activate methodology can be used through real-world use cases, with a comprehensive discussion on Agile and Scrum, in the context of SAP Project.

You will get familiar with SAP S4HANA which is an incredibly innovative platform for businesses which can store business data, interpret it, analyze it, process it in real time, and use it when it's needed depending upon the business requirement. This book articulates integration of SAP S/4HANA with Machine Learning Intelligence, intelligent enterprise tips & tricks, SAP Geographical Enablement Framework, Agricultural Contract Management, SAP Activate issues and challenges in large, mid and small scale projects and mitigation plan, Fit/Gap Workshops, Master Data Management, Vendor-Managed Inventory, useful Tips and Tricks for successful implementation of any Greenfield or brownfield, use of Agile, Scrum, Kanban, XP in SAP S/4 HANA Project and contains 400

PLUS Real-time SAP Activate & SAP S/4 HANA Interview questions and answers.

It's a journey, not a silver bullet, and leaders need to avoid getting caught in analysis paralysis. Start making the changes, get the wins and let the organization evolve.

– Melissa Sargeant

The book features more on practical approach with more examples covering topics from simple to complex one addressing many of the core concepts and advance topics also.

It is said *To err is human, to forgive divine.* Although the book is written with sincerity and honesty but in this light, I wish that the shortcomings of the book will be forgiven. At the same time the author is open to any kind of constructive criticisms and suggestions for further improvement. All intelligent suggestions are welcome and the author will try their best to incorporate such in valuable suggestions in the subsequent editions of this book.

Acknowledgement

No task is a single man's effort. Cooperation and Coordination of various people at different levels go into successful implementation of this book.

There is always a sense of gratitude, which everyone expresses others for their helpful and needy services they render during difficult phases of life and to achieve the goal already set.

At the outset I am thankful to the almighty that is constantly and invisibly guiding everybody and have also helped me to work on the right path.

I am son of Retired Professor (*Shri Ganesh Chandra Malakar*). I am indebted to my Father as without his support it was not possible to reach this Milestone. My loving mother (*Smt. Sikha Malakar*) always provides inspiration to me. My cute loving Son (*Master Shreyan Malakar*) is always providing me precious support at his level best.

I am thankful to my parents, spouse, son and family for their guidance which motivated me to work for the betterment of consultants by writing the book with sincerity and honesty. Without their support, this book was not possible.

I wish my sincere thanks to colleagues who helped and kept me motivated for writing this text.

We also thank the Publisher and the whole staff at BPB Publication, especially *Mr. Manish Jain* for motivation and for bringing this text in a nice presentable form.

Finally, I thank everyone who has directly or indirectly contributed to complete this authentic work.

About the Author

Sudipta Malakar is an accomplished IT SAP Project Manager, Program Manager, Agile Coach with more than fifteen years of experience in directing SAP DEV teams in supporting many major fortune 500 clients in multiple large accounts that include more than seven years of experience in IT Project/Program & Solution Delivery Management and more than five years of experience in Agile as SCRUM Master, Agile Coach.

He is certified Disruptive Strategy professional from HBX Harvard Business School, USA, Bachelor degree in Technology (B. TECH) in Chemical Technology from Calcutta University.

He is certified Sr. Project Manager in (Prince-2), CSP®, CSM®, KMP, ICP-ACC®, TKP®, ITIL, DevOps, ISO, Lean Six Sigma Black Belt, CMMi.

Table of Content

Introduction

It has been a general observation that most SAP consultants and professionals are used to the conventional waterfall methodology. SAP Activate is an innovative, next generation business suite that allows producing working deliverables straight away.

The traditional Waterfall model has many pitfalls in current market with varying complex customer requirements. SAP Activate Methodology is a harmonized agile implementation approach for cloud, on premise, and hybrid deployments for delivering shippable product increments in an iterative and incremental way. The SAP Activate methodology contains accelerators, tools, templates, questionnaires, checklists, work streams and guidebooks to ensure efficient, consistent, and repeatable delivery of SAP implementations and upgrades. As a successor to traditional implementation methodology, SAP Activate is underused, generally as a little material has been published on the modular and agile framework.

Manage your SAP Project with SAP Activate, will take your learning to the next level. The book promises to make you understand and practice the SAP Activate Framework. The focus is to take you on a journey of all the phases of SAP Activate methodology and make you understand all the phases with real life examples, lessons learnt, accelerators, and best practices. Well articulation on how SAP Activate methodology can be used through real-world use cases, with a comprehensive discussion on Agile and Scrum, in the context of SAP Project.

You will get familiar with SAP S4HANA which is an incredibly innovative platform for businesses which can store business data, interpret it, analyze it, process it in real time, and use it when it's needed depending upon the business requirement. This book articulates integration of SAP S/4HANA with Machine Learning Intelligence, intelligent enterprise tips & tricks, SAP Geographical Enablement Framework, Agricultural Contract Management, SAP Activate issues and challenges in large, mid and small scale Projects and mitigation plan, Fit/Gap Workshops, Master Data Management, Vendor-Managed Inventory, useful Tips & Tricks for successful implementation of any Greenfield or brownfield, use of Agile, Scrum, Kanban, XP in SAP S/4 HANA Project and contains 400 PLUS

Real-time SAP Activate & SAP S/4 HANA Interview questions and answers.

"It's a journey, not a silver bullet, and leaders need to avoid getting caught in analysis paralysis. Start making the changes, get the wins and let the organization evolve."

–Melissa Sargeant

The book has been written in such a way that the concepts are explained in detail, giving adequate emphasis on real-life examples.

Target audience for this book may be in IT domain having software background, preferably with SAP technical or techno functional or functional or domain knowledge. Designed to explore the challenges, critical issues, and opportunities arising from SAP Activate methodology and Agile practices, SAP Activate helps Project Managers, SAP consultants, and team members to make full use of Agile Scrum software development processes for successful implementation of any Green field or brown field implementation projects or migration or upgrade projects.

The book features more on practical approach with more examples covering topics from simple to complex one addressing many of the core concepts and advance topics also.

The book is divided into the following sections:

- 410 PLUS Real-time SAP Activate & SAP S/4 HANA Interview questions and answers
- Numerous Tricky Real-time SAP Activate Case Studies and Demos
- SAP S/4 HANA – Approach & Guidelines
- Explore the application scenarios of SAP Activate
- SAP Activate issues and challenges in large, mid, and small scale Projects and mitigation plan
- Useful Tips & Tricks for successful implementation of any green field or brown field implementation projects or migration or upgrade projects
- Digital transformation tips & tricks
- Intelligent enterprise tips & tricks
- Integration of SAP S/4HANA with Machine Learning Intelligence
- Agricultural Contract Management
- SAP Geographical Enablement Framework

- Explore the three pillars of SAP Activate and see how it works in different scenarios
- Understand and Implement Agile, Scrum, Kanban, XP concepts in SAP Activate
- Get to crisp with SAP Activate framework and manage your SAP projects effectively
- Agile prioritization technique
- Integration – SAP Solution Manager and SAP Activate
- SAP Activate – Governance, Roles and Responsibilities
- SAP Activate – Guiding principles and Critical success factors
- SAP Activate, ASAP and SAP Launch – Comparison
- SAP Activate Methodology – Quality Built-In and 10 quality principles
- Fit/Gap Workshops
- Validation and delta Workshops
- Project accelerators in SAP Activate methodology
- Real-time use cases & architecture in SAP HANA
- ECC and SAP HANA – Comparison
- Inventory Management – Data Model Redesign in S/4 HANA
- Fiori
- Sales Data model simplification in SAP S/4 HANA
- Mapping of key Innovations to Product Map in SAP S/4 HANA
- Project Governance - In an Agile context
- Supply-Chain-Planning Overview in S/4 HANA and SCM
- Use of SAP S/4HANA in Enterprise Management
- S/4 HANA Conversion paths – from Business Suite to S/4 HANA
- Nuts & Bolts of SAP Activate Methodology and S/4 HANA
- Mission Control Centre (MCC)
- Operations Control Centre (OCC)
- Innovation Control Centre (ICC)
- Integration validation (IV)

CHAPTER 1

SAP Activate Methodology - Introduction

SAP Activate is the first Agile and S4/HANA focused methodology for SAP projects. It is one simple, modular and agile methodology supporting all S/4 HANA transition scenarios. This book will provide you with detailed training to make you an expert in the methodology and enable you to use the Agile Methodology on your SAP project immediately.

In short, SAP Activate is a combination of SAP Best Practices, SAP guided configuration, and agile methodology which allows building smart and simplify the adoption of SAP S/4 HANA. SAP Activate gives the freedom to run fast with Fiori UX and with a lower TCO and continuous innovation with built-in extensibility to fit different needs. The key take away will be that SAP Activate is one methodology for any deployment mode - cloud, hybrid, on premise, or mobile for S\4 HANA.

It provides best practices for migration, integration and configuration for SAP S/4 HANA. It supports different starting points for customers to adopt SAP S/4 HANA – new implementation, system conversion and landscape transformation.

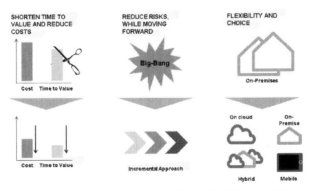

Figure 1.1 Purpose and goals of SAP Activate
Image Source: SAP SE / AG

The figure shows the key shift that we are seeing in the delivery of projects. The left side of the figure represents the continuous push for lower costs of implementation and compressed time to value (which you can also approximate with the time it takes to deploy the solutions into production environment). The pace of change is increasing and there is more pressure to deliver the projects faster.

Another change we have seen is the shift from the big-bang deployment projects to more focused projects that are implemented incrementally in multiple releases. In this new environment, customers are also looking to implement projects in a shorter time line with accelerators and with jump-start content that they can start with.

Customers are also looking for a higher flexibility in choices for solution deployment - ranging from deployment in the cloud, on-premise, hybrid, and access to information on mobile devices.

To meet this demand, SAP now offers the ability to deploy and manage solutions in the cloud, on-premise, and in the hybrid environment. SAP also offers mobile access to solution capabilities.

There are many advantages in deploying the solutions in the cloud.

Main Characteristics of Cloud

- Deliver value quickly
- Co-Innovate with customer by constantly pursuing new technologies like HANA
- Drive customer satisfaction and solution adoption
- Establish efficient engagement governance

With 'Cloud', SAP takes care of system requirements and maintenance. Customers can take advantage of the latest innovations through automatic quarterly updates. With Cloud, customers are up and running quickly, while SAP takes care of future upgrades and enhancements. An implementation methodology helps you minimize risk and streamline and accelerate your project. An advantage of cloud projects is reduced implementation costs and durations – reducing the total implementation time from several years to a few months. With Cloud, functionality is configured in iterations and multi-release schedules instead of all the functionality in a big bang approach. Multi-release schedules may also mean roll-out of functionality from country to country or business organization to business organization instead of everyone at the same time. For cloud implementations, the

Agile methodology approach may be a better framework than the classical on-premise waterfall methodologies.

With cloud implementation methodology you can take a disciplined project management approach to your implementation, migration, and change projects.

SAP Activate has following three key elements:

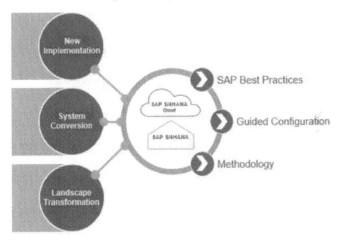

Figure 1.2 The three Pillars of SAP Activate
Image Source: SAP SE / AG

1) SAP Best Practices

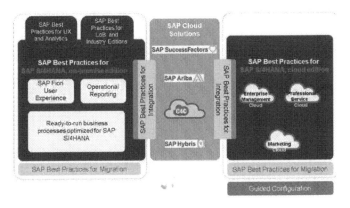

Figure 1.3 Portfolio of SAP S/4HANA Best Practices for
SAP solutions, integration, and master data
Image Source: SAP SE / AG

The preceding figure shows some of the Best Practices for SAP solutions, integration, and master data.

These ready-to-run business processes are easily integrated.

The best practices packages are available in the SAP Service Marketplace. Customers can download the SAP Best Practices content and use it in their own environment. For Cloud implementations, the Best Practices processes will be pre-activated when the cloud solution is provisioned.

- Business Process Structure with technical steps that include finance and logistical areas.
- Accelerators for your implementation project.
- Integration information with other cloud solutions, such as Success Factors Employee Central or Ariba Network.
- Migration documents which help to migrate either from Non SAP systems or from legacy SAP systems.
- Graphical representation of all the business processes.
- Pre-defined test scripts.
- Testing automation process available in S\4 HANA.

SAP activate has improvements in the following areas:

- Based on use of SAP Best Practices
- Reduced project lifecycle - only four phases
- Up to 10 key deliverables per phase, thus easier access to key guides and accelerators
- Blueprint activities replaced with solution validation
- Agile implementation as a default

2) Guided Configuration

SAP Activate was introduced as an adoption framework for SAP S/4 HANA. In the on-premise implementation, the project teams will use the IMG (Implementation Guide or SPRO) tools to configure the solution.

3) One Methodology

SAP Activate has following four phases:

1. **Prepare:** Start with best practices by re-using knowledge assets and prebuild content.

2. **Explore:** Moving into pre assembly, rapid prototyping, solution validation workshops and delta backlog.

3. **Realize:** In this phase iterative delta scope implementation and E2E integration testing.

4. **Deploy:** This is the final phase where the roll out is done.

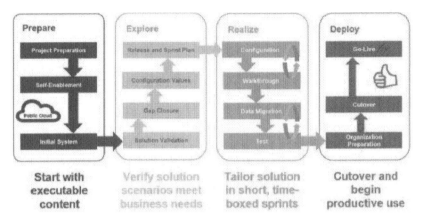

Figure 1.4 SAP Activate high level summary
Image Source: SAP SE / AG

SAP Activate for new implementation of SAP Ariba High Level Summary.

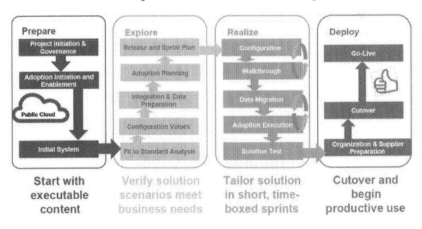

Figure 1.5 SAP Activate for new implementation of SAP Ariba high level summary
Image Source: SAP SE / AG

SAP Activate is an implementation framework consisting of SAP Best Practices, Guided Configuration, and Methodology. SAP Activate can be used when only one application is being implemented as well as when many solutions are implemented within one project.

SAP Activate can be used for on-premise, hybrid, and cloud implementations.

It can be used when only one application is being implemented as well as when many solutions are implemented within one project.

It can be used for projects managed by customers, SAP Professional Services or SAP Partner. This provides a common approach so that all members of the implementation team know what they will do and when.

Example use:

On-Premise: Used for implementation of S/4 HANA On-Premise editions and other SAP applications.

Cloud: Used for implementation of S/4 HANA Cloud edition, SAP SuccessFactors, and other SAP applications.

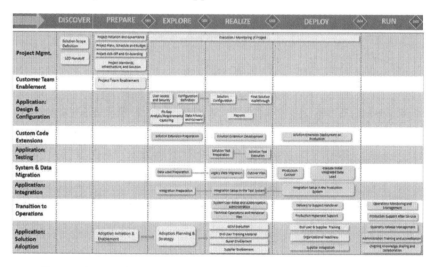

Figure 1.5 Deliverables / activities across the workstreams in
SAP Activate Methodology
Image Source: SAP SE / AG

Agile Build Iterations with Incremental Configurations

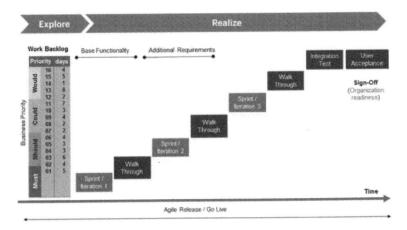

Figure 1.6 Agile Build: Iterative iterations with incremental configurations
Image Source SAP SE / AG

Using MoSCoW prioritization technique we are setting priority of different business requirements within the EXPLORE phase.

MoSCoW prioritization technique

Letter	Stands for	Which means
M	Must Have	• Minimum set of essential requirements, without which the system would be useless (MMF). • All of these requirements must be satisfied.
S	Should Have	• Important requirements for which there is a short-term work-around. The system is useful without them. • These requirements can be included in the initial project scope, but may be removed from the project scope to accommodate changed requirements.
C	Could Have	• These requirements are valuable and nice-to-have, but can easily be left out of the solution. • These requirements may be left out of the initial scope of the release in order to accommodate a time constraint.
W	Would Have/ Won't have	• Time-permitting. • As changes to requirements or project progress dictates, lower priority requirements may be removed from the scope of the project.

Within REALIZE Phase we will have sprints or iterations.

Agile development manages on *Sprints*. It means that the time table is much shorter (less than 30 days) and several products features are to be produced and released in that period.

A Scrum Sprint is a repeatable cycle during which work is completed and made ready for review. The duration of the Scrum Sprint depends on the size of the project and the team working on it. Generally, it is under 30 days.

SAP S/4 HANA - The Next Generation Business Suite

Figure 1.7 SAP S/4 HANA - The next generation business suite
Image Source SAP SE / AG

SAP S/4 HANA was introduced to the market in 2015. It has been introduced as a re-imaged Business Suite that represents the core for customers' business and is based on a SAP HANA platform with SAP Fiori UX (making it easy for people to access and use the solution). This enterprise core system is then connected to the solutions that help companies in managing people, managing big data, connecting to the business network, managing the Internet of Things, and other capabilities. SAP offers integrated solutions for companies running various aspects of their businesses ranging from SAP Ariba to Concur, SAP Fieldglass, SAP SuccessFactors, and SAP Hybris solutions.

1.1 SAP Activate – The Three Pillars

SAP Activate has the following three key elements:

1) SAP Best Practices

- SAP delivers ready-to-run business processes that are optimized for SAP S/4 HANA containing OLTP and OLAP, delivered with the product.
- It has best practices for integration, migration, and extensibility to expand the existing processes with the customer's own processes.
- It has delivery of a reference solution in the cloud for a fast start.
- Continuous process of improvement of SAP SuccessFactors Best Practices

It has the following aspects:

(a) **Fast time to value**

- Deploy SAP innovations fast, simple, and flexible
- Get a jump-start for your implementations with SAP best practices

(b) **Predictable results**

- Leverage preconfigured business content
- Use SAP's tested and proven methodology with prescriptive guidelines

(c) **Simple On-boarding to cloud**

- Protect on-premise investments with extensions to the cloud
- Move up on the path to the cloud from pre-assembled pilots to productive use

SAP Best Practices help project teams accelerate time to value. They provide content that helps jump-start the implementation with read-to-run processes and other assets.

The Best Practices contain rich business scenarios and business content. This helps customers get predictable and repeatable results from the Best Practices. The Best Practices and some additional set up, (for example, personalization, additional configuration or enhancements of the pre-delivered content), can be used as a baseline for an implementation project.

Best Practices can be deployed in the cloud which further improves flexibility and time to value.

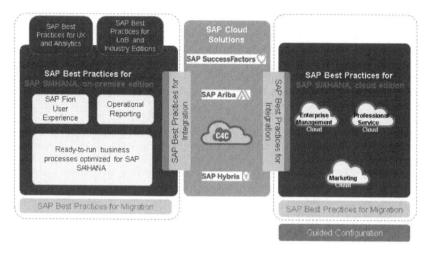

Figure 1.8 Portfolio of SAP S/4HANA Best Practices overview
Image Source: SAP SE / AG

The figure shows some of the Best Practices for SAP S/4 HANA.

SAP Best Practices for SAP S/4 HANA provide ready-to-run digitized analytical and operational business processes that cover the fundamental business processes of an enterprise, often referred to as the baseline. No matter if you want to streamline your procure to pay processes, optimize your order to cash flow, or take advantage of simple finance, we provide a pre-configuration for many of your business priorities.

Let's take a look at an example of a new financial implementation. You can leverage parallel accounting to address multinational reporting requirements; deliver standard chart of accounts; preconfigured best practice solution for closing books, remaining IFRS compliant, tracking debits and credits, calculating taxes.

These ready-to-run business processes are easily integrated with other cloud solutions, such as SAP SuccessFactors Employee Central or the Ariba Network. SAP provides Best Practices for integration with cloud solutions.

SAP offers a set of best practices content for line of business and industry solutions that are available for our customers to leverage and integrate with their SAP S/4HANA Solution.

SAP delivers Best Practices for user experience with SAP Fiori.

The best practices packages are available in the SAP Service Marketplace. Customers can download the SAP Best Practices content and use it in their own environment. For Cloud implementations, the Best Practices processes will be pre-activated when the cloud solution is provisioned.

2) Guided Configuration

- The guided configuration system is now available in the cloud.
- For customers or expert users who can command and configure a solution, there are tools for an assisted implementation that provide a self-service configuration user experience.
- These tools empower business users to configure the environment and make it much easier to configure. The configuration tables are in IMG.
- The guided configuration also offers capabilities for what we call content lifecycle management. This essentially involves looking at the configuration settings and ensuring that the configuration settings that are set in that solution are not impacted by a new version of best practices or a new version of processes that are being shipped in the next release of the SAP solution. This is extremely important in the cloud where the release cycle is much more compressed.
- SAP S/4HANA comes with new capabilities and new functionality every quarter. The pace of change and innovation that the customers are getting through the cloud solutions is much higher than what we would see with on-premise solutions. So with cloud solutions it is important to use the guided configuration tools.

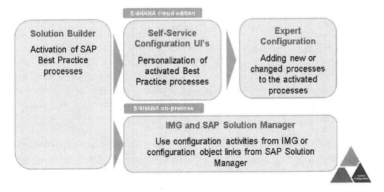

Figure 1.9 Portfolio of SAP S/4HANA guided configuration overview
Image Source: SAP SE / AG

SAP Activate Guided configuration is a new approach for an assisted way to implement SAP Best Practices. For SAP S/4HANA Cloud edition, it also facilitates the lifecycle management of the pre-configured business processes from SAP and any additional customizing added by the customer. SAP is providing various tools to support these efforts.

Tools to assist rapid implementation such as SAP SuccessFactors Administration Tool and Setup Wizards.

Historical content awareness – know content and context of successive configuration, integration, and value delivery projects.

We recognize two cases of how the configuration tools are used with SAP S/4HANA:

- The implementation of SAP S/4HANA cloud solution
- And implementation of the on-premise solution

Both start with using the Solution Builder tool to activate the Best Practices.

Next steps are then different in the on-premise and cloud. Let's cover each case separately starting with cloud:

SAP S/4HANA Cloud

- The activated environment can be adjusted with the self-service configuration UIs that are available to a customer or partner to use to configure and personalize the solution.

- The expert configuration capabilities are available for deeper configuration changes and access to this environment is restricted to SAP Service Center. The Service Center team works with the customer or with the implementation partner to apply the desired configuration settings in the system.

SAP S/4HANA on-premise

- In on-premise deployment, the project team uses the pre-activate Best Practices content in the sandbox system. SAP recommends using the pre-activated SAP S/4HANA software appliance deployed into AWS for purposes of fit/gap analysis which we will cover later in the course. Then the on-premise project team uses the standard implementation guide for configuration. The team also uses SAP Solution Manager to capture and store the solution documentation in one central place.

SAP solution builder tool

- This tool is used to develop and structure configuration content according to the domain model of SAP.

- All processes are modeled as scope items. Scope items are implemented through building blocks.

- Content is not just an option, but an integral part of the product. SAP solution builder tool is used to activate this SAP Best Practices content in the customer system.

Self Service Configuration UIs (relevant for SAP S/4HANA Cloud editions)

- Next to the activation of ready-to-run business processes delivered by SAP Best Practices, customers typically want to personalize processes.

- Personalization typically does not change a business process but adjusts settings to the customer needs.

- SAP provides easy to use SAP Fiori applications for self-service configurations to support personalization.

Expert Configuration (relevant for SAP S/4HANA Cloud editions)

- Our experience has taught us that almost no customer project can be implemented without adjustments.

- Customers typically want to add new processes or adjust pre-configured business processes delivered by SAP Activate.

- SAP will make Expert Configuration available to support these needs.

- With expert configuration you can create your own scope items and (delta) building block(s) for any complementary content development at your side.

IMG and SAP Solution Manager

Use configuration activities from the product **Implementation Guide (IMG)** or configuration object links added to the Configuration documentation in SAP Solution Manager.

Guided Configuration Overview

Guided configurations are tools and accelerators that allow customers to be more self-sufficient. Guided Configurations enable you to:

- Configure your solution

- Test your process
- Migrate your data

Tools and Accelerators

Examples of Guided Configurations are as follows:

- SAP SuccessFactors Administration Tools
- SAP SuccessFactors Wizards
- SAP SuccessFactors Migration Templates

Self Sufficiency

Self-sufficiency allows projects to be faster as work can be more decentralized. Changes can be implemented and tested with higher quality as the guided configuration can have pre-built in checks.

3) One Methodology / SAP Activate Methodology

- The methodology is the third component or pillar of SAP Activate.
- Processes to guide the customer through the implementation. Agile methodology for rapid delivery and quality control. One agile methodology for any deployment mode (cloud, hybrid, on-premise, mobile), rapid delivery, and quality control: PREPARE, EXPLORE, REALIZE, DEPLOY.
- We are starting with a working system based on best practices and one of the big pillars that we are using is agile techniques to support the implementation.
- We are supporting all different types of deployments into the Cloud, on-premise, and the hybrid deployment.
- The core of the methodology is that the project starts with the Prepare phase and goes into the Explore, Realize, and Deploy phases. So we have four phases.
- We have incorporated many terms and approaches from the learnings that we have made in SAP Cloud solutions and those that SAP acquired in the cloud and brought that experience into the methodology.
- SAP Activate succeeded in both SAP methodology and SAP Launch methodology in the cloud.
- We also have enhanced support for premium engagements. Premium engagements are for the types of services that SAP Services offers to our customers for safeguarding, planning and implementing

technology or implementing the functionality. We have specific plug-ins into the methodology to highlight where the services are applicable.

Methodology Overview

Full support is available in SAP Activate Methodology for initial deployments as well as continuous business adoption and innovation with a unified implementation approach for cloud, hybrid deployments and on-Premise.

ASAP Methodology

The ASAP methodology is the successor of ASAP (Accelerated SAP) and SAP Launch methodologies, combining the best of each into SAP Activate.

Agile Methodology

SAP Activate is based on an Agile methodology approach emphasizing iterations or sprints of configuration and walkthroughs and iterations of Go-Live release cycles.

This methodology is the successor of ASAP (Accelerated SAP) and SAP Launch methodologies, combining the best of each into SAP Activate.

SAP Activate is based on an Agile methodology approach emphasizing iterations or sprints of configuration and walkthroughs and iterations of Go-Live release cycles.

SAP Activate Methodology provides full support for initial deployments as well as continuous business adoption and innovation with a harmonized implementation approach for cloud, on-premise, and hybrid deployments.

SAP Activate Methodology was designed for implementations of S/4HANA on-premise, S/4HANA cloud, and most importantly with SAP SuccessFactors in mind.

SAP Activate Methodology has 4 phases similar to SAP Launch. The four phases are called PREPARE, EXPLORE, REALIZE, and DEPLOY.

During the PREPARE Phase, activities occur to ensure that the project is ready to be executed efficiently. During the EXPLORE Phase, activities occur to ensure all the specifications for the configuration, migration, and interfaces are well-defined. During the Realize Phase, activities occur to complete the configuration, migration steps, interface set up, and the end-to-end solution is fully tested. During the DEPLOY Phase, activities occur to move the solution into Production and ensure processes and people are in place to support the application after Go-Live.

1.2 SAP Solution Manager and SAP Activate

SAP Solution Manager 7.2, an integrated platform, drives the unified solution of IT business processes to deliver a unique outcome catering the business needs.

It can also be referred to as the *ERP for your IT*.

Figure 1.10 SAP Solution Manager 7.2 and SAP Activate integration
Image Source: SAP SE / AG

Portfolio to Project (P2P) balances business initiatives and values vs. information technology capacity, skills and timelines, drives the portfolio of projects

a. It balances business initiatives and values versus information technology capacity, skills, and timelines

b. Provides an integrated viewpoint across PMO, enterprise architecture, and service portfolio

c. Improves data quality for decision-making

d. Improve business communication by providing KPIs and roadmaps

Requirement- to- Deploy (R2D) builds what and when business needs it with measured business outcome:

a. Provides a framework for enhancing, creating or sourcing a service

b. Supports different development methodologies (like, agile and traditional waterfall)

c. Enables transparency of the deliverables / products / services quality, utility, schedule, and cost

d. Defines continuous integration & deployment touch points

Request to Fulfill (R2F) to request, catalog and fulfill services:

a. Helps your IT organization transformation to a service model

b. From multiple supplier catalogs, presents a single catalog with items

c. Efficiently manages subscriptions and value for money

d. Effectively manages realizations across multiple service providers

Detect to Correct (D2C) to resolve and anticipate production problems:

a. Enhances results and efficiency by bringing together IT service operations

b. Enables end-to-end visibility using a shared guided configuration model

c. Identifies issues before they affect users

d. Reduces the mean time to repair

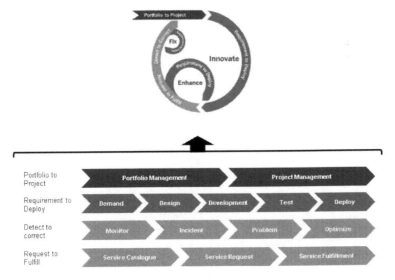

Figure 1.11 Detect to Correct (D2C) overview
Image Source: SAP SE / AG

SAP Solution Manager provides support to the following processes:

a. Process management

b. Test Suite

c. Project Management

d. Business process Operations

e. Data Volume Management

f. Change Control Management

g. IT Service management

h. Custom Code management

i. Landscape Management.

SAP Solution Manager 7.2 - Branches

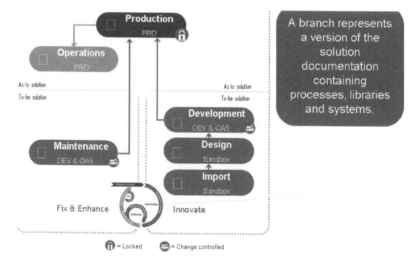

Figure 1.12 SAP Solution Manager 7.2 - Branches

Image Source: SAP SE / AG

For these value assurance packages, SAP Solution Manager is delivering infrastructure:

1. SAP Solution Manager 7.2 performs the following activities once a customer has signed up for Premium Engagements service:

    a. From SAP Cloud downloads a project plan, it is adapted to the business' needs during the planning workshop. For SAP

S/4HANA, for new installation, conversion, and landscape transformation is available: SAP S/4HANA Transition it provides a unified project plan.

   b. Orchestrates the service delivery.

   c. Synchronizes Q-Gates with SAP's back office.

2. SAP Solution Manager 7.2 does the following in the prepare/explore phase:

   a. From the SAP Cloud for build and design, it imports business processes

   b. With fully activated configuration based on SAP Activate content and DBS model companies it manages delta scoping using a live SAP S/4HANA trial system

   c. Manages customers' business requirements from fit/gap analysis till implementation

3. SAP Solution Manager 7.2 does the following in the realize/deploy phase:

   a. Breaks down requirements into work packages and assigns them to waves.

   b. Giving delivery of shippable deliverables in iterative and incremental way in sprints based on business priority.

   c. Reports the build progress automatically.

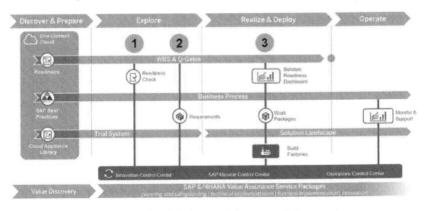

Figure 1.13 SAP Solution Manager 7.2 overview

Image Source: SAP SE / AG

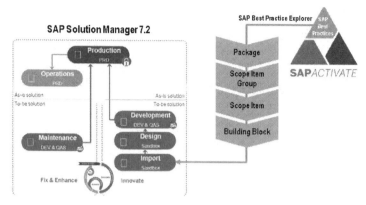

Figure 1.14 SAP Solution Manager 7.2 integration with SAP Activate

Image Source: SAP SE / AG

From the Roadmap Viewer you can download the roadmap content. One file type from the download can be uploaded to SAP Solution Manager 7.2 as an IT PPM Project.

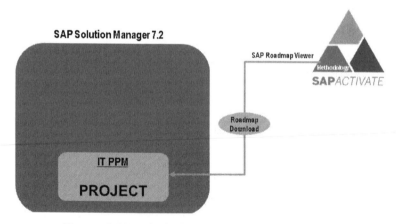

Figure 1.15 Interlinking of Roadmap Viewer and
SAP Solution Manager 7.2

Image Source: SAP SE / AG

For SAP S/4HANA solutions the SAP Activate Configuration tools refers to the Configuration Library in SAP Solution Manager 7.2; from there the Configuration object links can be used to define configuration activities such as using a classic IMG Object.

For the configuration of SAP S/4HANA Cloud solution we do not use SAP Solution manager and instead use the Guided Configuration tools available to *Manage Solution*.

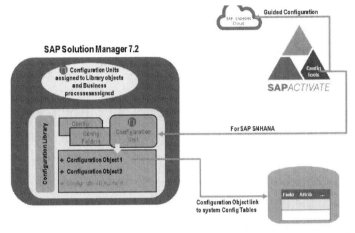

Figure 1.16 Guided Configuration and SAP S/4HANA interlinking

Image Source: SAP SE / AG

SAP Activate and SAP Solution Manager 7.2 support the transition to SAP S/4HANA.

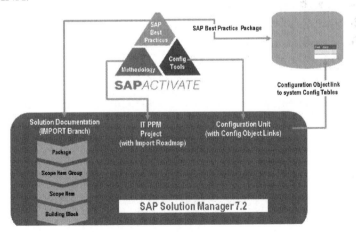

Figure 1.17 SAP S/4HANA transition via SAP Activate and SAP Solution Manager 7.2

Image Source: SAP SE / AG

1.3 SAP Activate – Key Characteristics

1. Start with best practices:

   Use Ready-to-run business processes

2. Cloud Ready:

   Leverage the flexibility and speed of the cloud

3. Validate Solution:

   Validate to best practices with fit/gap workshops to capture delta

4. Premium engagement ready:

   Build and run fully supported via SAP control centers

5. Modular, scalable and Agile:

   Structure project to deliver the solution iteratively and incrementally

6. Quality Built-in:

   Identify risk early with total quality approach

Benefits

The following points, on SAP Activate Methodology Benefits, provide a summary of the benefits of the SAP Activate methodology.

- Enable consistent project delivery, reduce complexity, and increases quality by providing common framework and language for all SAP project

- Broad product coverage, including support for SAP SuccessFactors and all transition scenarios to SAP S/4HANA

- Scalable, supports all size of projects, from small fast cloud deployments to comprehensive global deployments in an on-premise and hybrid environment

- Prescriptive and comprehensive – provides guided work procedures for project team members, deliverables for project managers and accelerators like how-to documents and templates for all users

- Accelerates project delivery through use of SAP Best Practices, fit/gap analysis, Agile project management, application visualization, and use of Cloud technology

- Methodology foundation fully aligned with proven project management practice of Project Management Institute, like formal Quality, Risk, and Issues Management

1.4 SAP Activate – Structure

Phases are stages of the project. At the end of each phase, a quality gate exists to verify the completion of the deliverables.

A Workstream is a collection of related deliverables that show time relationships within a project and among other streams. Streams can span phases and are not necessarily dependent on phase starts and ends.

A deliverable is an outcome that is delivered during the course of the project. Several deliverables are included within a stream.

A task is work to be performed. One or several tasks comprise a deliverable.

The figure above, Methodology Breakdown, shows the taxonomy of the SAP Activate methodology. It consists of several elements. We will discuss each element individually and in the context of how they work together.

The structural elements are as follows:

a. Phase

b. Deliverable

c. Task

In addition to these structural elements, the SAP Activate methodology contains workstreams which are assigned as an attribute to deliverables and tasks.

Phases are stages of the project. At the end of each phase, a quality gate exists to verify the completion of the deliverables.

A deliverable is an outcome that is delivered during the course of the project. Several deliverables are included within a workstream.

A task is work to be performed. One or several tasks comprise a deliverable.

The workstream is an attribute assigned to deliverables and tasks. A workstream represents a collection of related deliverables that show time relationships within a project and among other streams. Streams can span phases and are not necessarily dependent on phase starts and ends.

Each workstream has deliverables or a set of deliverables. These outcomes are delivered during the course of the project. There are multiple deliverables that are assigned to the workstream and each deliverable is then broken down into individual tasks.

Tasks represent the work or the activities that the project team performs. A group of tasks leads to the creation of the deliverable, which represents a tangible outcome that is handed over to the customer, or it may be an interim outcome in the context of the project.

SAP ACTIVATE for New Implementation of SAP SuccessFactors: High-Level Summary

This slide provides a simplified high-level summary of selected activities in the implementation of SAP SuccessFactors that can be used as part of an introduction to the project approach with SAP Activate.

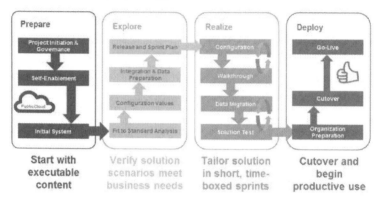

Figure 1.18 SAP Activate for new implementation high level summary
Image Source: SAP SE / AG

SAP Activate Methodology for SuccessFactors: Deliverable per Phase

The following image shows the deliverables defined within the solution specific SAP Activate methodology for the implementation of SAP SuccessFactors.

Figure 1.19 SAP Activate phase wise deliverables
Image Source: SAP SE / AG

Under Realize phase, after legacy data migration the following deliverables are present generally:

- Solution Test Execution
- System user roles and Authorization administration
- Technical operations and handover plan
- Cutover plan
- Phase closure

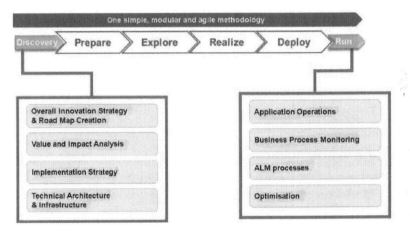

Figure 1.20 Additional phases of SAP Activate overview
Image Source: SAP SE / AG

The figure above, Additional Phases, shows two additional phases that are often referenced:

The DISCOVERY phase where the deliverables can be leveraged to build a business case for a SAP-based solution implementation programme / project.

The RUN phase represents the deliverables and tasks to run and operate the SAP solution.

DISCOVERY phase deliverables include:

Figure 1.21 Discovery phase deliverables overview
Image Source: SAP SE / AG

In the first deliverable customers create an overall company strategy for their digital transformation – this can include SAP S/4HANA as the digital core, but looks from a broader perspective.

Key topics like Internet of things, Big Data, Smart Data, Omni-channel, or Business Networks can also be captured in the strategy.

RUN phase deliverables reflect supporting the system operations and improvements that are not their own project:

Application Operations – capabilities for monitoring systems, alerting, analysis, and administration of SAP solutions; helping bring control and lower TCO

Business Process Monitoring – monitoring specific process metrics or interfaces and providing analytics for review

ALM processes – small enhancements and fixes to the solution outside a major project release; change management of software and documentation

Optimization – through focused services in response to problem trends

1) DISCOVER Phase

The purpose of the DISCOVER phase is for the customer to come to understand the breath, depth, and functionality of the SAP SuccessFactors solution. Within this phase, the customer and implementation team will discuss the overall HR strategy, business drivers and priorities, key success metrics, specified solution scope and HR Business processes, functionality requirements, and work on an initial implementation scenario.

During this phase, the customer and the sales team come to a jointly-agreed description of the implementation scope, overall project timelines, and target solution model.

2) PREPARE Phase

The purpose of this phase is to provide the initial planning and preparation for the project. In this phase, the project is started, plans are finalized, project team is assigned, and work is under way to start the project optimally.

Key PREPARE Activities:

- Define project goals, a high-level scope, and a project plan
- Identify and quantify business value objectives
- Secure executive sponsorship

- Establish project standards, organization, and governance
- Define and secure approval for the implementation/upgrade strategy
- Define roles and responsibilities for the project team
- Validate the project objectives
- Establish project management, tracking, and reporting mechanisms for value delivery
- Develop a project team training strategy and start project team training
- Document all initiation activities in the project charter
- Pre-assemble (or establish) the project environment, infrastructure, and IT systems including SAP Solution Manager
- Prepare for the EXPLORE phase

In the PREPARE phase, we have different accelerators including the following:

- Delivery supplement
- Solution scope document
- Software and delivery requirements for the Best Practices
- Work Breakdown Structure
- Project Management Plans and Governance documents

This is only a partial list of assets available for the team in the PREPARE phase.

3) EXPLORE Phase

The purpose of this phase is to perform a fit/gap analysis to validate the solution functionality included in the project scope and to confirm that the business requirements can be satisfied. Identified gaps and configuration values are added to the backlog for use in the next phase.

Key EXPLORE Phase Activities:

- Prepare, setup, and conduct solution validation workshops
- Refine business requirements
- Identify master data
- Confirm to be business processes

- Define functional solution design, including a gap analysis in solution design workshops
- Associate business requirements to the process hierarchy and the solution components
- Obtain business sign-off on delta requirements and design documents
- Collect end user information, analyze learning needs, and develop a learning deployment strategy
- Establish project management, tracking, and reporting for value delivery.

In the EXPLORE phase, we have different accelerators including the following:

- **Customer Presentation:** A master deck that covers the scope of the solution and the service.
- **Master Data Overview:** A table to understand the sample master data shipped in the package.
- **Organization Data Overview:** A table to understand the organization model data shipped in the package and how it relates to the software.
- **Process Diagrams:** A graphical representation of the steps in a scope item.
- **SAP Solution Manager Template:** A container for the implementation content for one or more solutions in an area.
- Project Backlog Template: Repository of all the data requirements and gaps to plan iterative, incremental build during REALIZE phase.

4) REALIZE Phase

The purpose of this phase is to use a series of iterations to incrementally build and test an integrated business and system environment that is based on the business scenarios and process requirements identified in the previous phase.

During this phase, data is loaded, adoption activities occur, and operations are planned.

Key REALIZE Phase Activities:

- Establish the solution landscape, implement the solution in the development environment using incremental build in time-boxed iterations
- Conduct overall end-to-end testing of the solution within the QA environment
- Prepare for data migration and data archiving
- Finalize end user training materials and documentation
- Track and report on value delivery during the REALIZE phase

In the REALIZE phase, we have different accelerators including the following:

- **Configuration Guides:** A detailed description of the required configuration.
- **Test Scripts:** A procedure for testing the activated system according to the defined best practices.
- **Agile Approach Guides:** Project team guides that explain how to structure project into releases and iterative sprints.
- **Cutover Plan:** Template for cutover planning and execution. Provides framework for transition to production.

The REALIZE phase moves towards using the configuration guides and test scripts. The team will be using the methodology guidance for Agile approach, and the guides for cutover planning. The cutover planning step is performed in the later part of this phase as the project moves towards the DEPLOY phase.

The project team actively works with business representatives to ensure a good fit of the built solution to the requirements from the backlog. Project team releases results of multiple iterations to the business users to accelerate time to value and provide early access to finalized functionality. Each release is thoroughly tested in end-to-end integration test and user acceptance test.

Agile Build: Iterative iterations with incremental configurations.

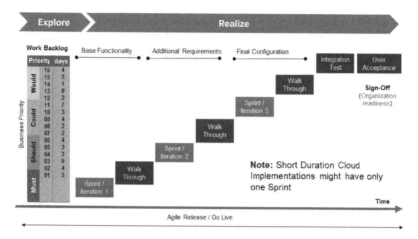

Figure 1.22 Iterative iterations with incremental configurations overview

Image Source: SAP SE / AG

Within the EXPLORE phase, we will document all the business requirements for the Release and assign them to different priorities.

Within the REALIZE Phase, we will have sprints or iterations. Each sprint or iteration consists of changes in configuration settings, changes in migration scripts, changes in interface set-up, and finally walkthroughs. Business requirements will be assigned to different iterations based upon priorities.

Usually in SAP SuccessFactors implementation projects there are three or fewer iterations.

Sprint 1: During **Iteration 1**, best practice content is usually activated

Sprint 2: During **Iteration 2**, the highest priority configurations and all changes from the best practice content are completed

Sprint 3: During **Iteration 3**, any changes discovered during **Iteration 2** walkthrough are corrected and all remaining configurations are completed

At the end of the last iteration, all the configuration settings have been set, the migration scripts have been completed, and the interfaces have been set up.

At the end of the REALIZE phase, the customer completes the integration and user acceptance testing.

5) DEPLOY Phase

The purpose of this phase is to setup the production system, confirm customer organization readiness, and to switch business operations to the new system.

Key DEPLOY Phase Activities:

Resolve all crucial open issues:

- Conduct system tests
- Check that system management is in place
- Proceed with cut-over activities, including data migration
- Execute transition and cutover plans including **organizational change management (OCM)** plans
- Complete all scheduled end-user training
- Identify and document all issues encountered in the transition to the new solution
- Monitor business process results and the production environment

Establish OCC** or an *"extra-care"* center of excellence for support that provides:

- Production support processes
- Exceptional business monitoring processes
- Extraordinary technical support
- System enhancements
- Track and report on value delivery

**This includes the Project Management Institute's A Guide to the Project Management Body of Knowledge.

In the DEPLOY phase, we have different accelerators including the following:

- **Project Schedule:** A basic project schedule that includes aggregated durations and a list of required skills/roles.
- **Cutover Plan:** A sample cutover schedule that provides list of cutover steps.
- **Operations Setup Guide:** Guide for setup of the operational support for solution after cutover to production.

In the DEPLOY phase, the team can find accelerators for the project schedule, detail Cutover plan and Cutover checklists as well as the operations set up guide that helps to set up the operations environment for running the solution.

1.5 SAP Best Practices Content

SAP Best Practices help project teams accelerate time to value. They provide content that helps jump-start the implementation with read-to-run processes and other assets. The Best Practices contain rich business scenarios and business content. This helps customers get predictable and repeatable results from the Best Practices. The Best Practices and some additional set up, (for example, personalization, additional configuration, or enhancements of the pre-delivered content), can be used as a baseline for an implementation project.

Best Practices can be deployed in the cloud which further improves flexibility and time to value.

Fast Time to Value

Implementations timelines can be dramatically shorten when customers use the Best Practices content as a starting point for their configuration settings.

- Get a jump-start for your implementations with SAP Best Practices for SAP SuccessFactors
- Deploy SAP SuccessFactors innovations fast, simple, and flexible

SAP Activate Best Practices

As a starting point for implementations, there are SAP Best Practices, as well as SAP Partners that may also have best practices content. SAP Best Practices content contains sample forms, sample test data, and more guidance. SAP Best Practices content is usually offered free of charge and can be found on SAP Marketplace or its successor.

Predictable Results

Once the best practices configuration settings have been installed, implementation projects can continue to refine the content and add additional configuration settings as required. Quality of projects can also increase as content has been pre-tested.

- Use SAP's tested and proven methodology with prescriptive guidelines

- Leverage pre-configured business content

Following is a list of some of the Best Practices related to SAP SuccessFactors.

Figure 1.23 SAP Best Practices for SAP SuccessFactors overview

Image Source: SAP SE / AG

Look at the SAP Best Practices Explorer (https://rapid.sap.com/bp/) to see the latest available content.

In May 2017, we could find the above content and Best Practices for integration such as:

- S/4HANA Cloud integration with SAP SuccessFactors employee central
- S/4HANA integration with SAP SuccessFactors employee central
- Employee central third-party Integration with SAP best practices

What's included with SAP SuccessFactors Best Practices:

Pre-configured Master Tenant

Pre-configured master tenant is a ready-to-run customer application with all the best practice content already configured. This ready to run application is usually activated for the customer during the PREPARE phase and used during the EXPLORE phase to demonstrate the starting point of configurations.

Configuration Guides

These are easy-to-use, step-by-step configuration guides for those customers that want to manually configure the system. One use case is for those customers already on SAP SuccessFactors that want to add additional modules and may want to manually configure the new module.

Configuration Workbook

Configuration workbook is a documentation of all the settings within the SAP Best Practices shown within Microsoft Excel spreadsheets. Customers can easily use these spreadsheets to confirm the settings and add additional customer specific settings. This is usually completed during the EXPLORE phase.

Demonstration Scripts

Demonstration scripts and demonstration tenants can be used during the EXPLORE phase to identify additional configuration that is needed beyond the Best Practices content.

Sample Test Data

Sample test data and process steps are provided so that testing by SAP and/or the customer can be accelerated. It contains pre-built trackers for capturing testing results.

Process Diagrams

Many customers want to document their HR processes. SAP Best Practices already contain the processes in process diagrams. These diagrams can be compared to customer requirements or used as a starting point for the final process flows for the customer solution.

Sample HR Forms

Sample HR Forms are provided so that the testing process can be accelerated. Many SAP SuccessFactors modules use forms built in XML format. SAP Best Practices already have many examples of forms in xml format that customers can use as-is or modify for their unique requirements.

SAP Best Practices Content in three layers

The *solution layer* corresponds to a specific version of the software that SAP is shipping for SAP S/4HANA, (for example, SAP S/4HANA, SAP S/4HANA Marketing Cloud, and so on). Within the solution, we can find scope items.

Examples of accelerators that are delivered:

- Customer presentation
- Sales supplement
- Software and delivery requirements
- Project schedule
- Solution scope
- Organizational data overview
- Master data overview

Scope items represent the predefined business processes like make-to-stock production process, sales order processing, and revenue planning process, to name a few. Each scope item represents the best practices functionality that is delivered out of the box. Scope items can be included or excluded from the project's scope.

Examples of accelerators that are delivered:

- Scope-item fact sheets
- Process diagrams
- Test scripts
- Scope-item simulations

The *building blocks* are actual configuration steps that set up the capability of the solution in the system. The configuration content is entered into these building blocks and executing the building blocks in the right sequence configures the best practices solution.

Examples of accelerators that are delivered:

- Building-block fact sheets
- Configuration guides
- Activation content

In Q3 2016, the SAP Best Practices content was made available in the SAP Best Practices Explorer (https://rapid.sap.com/bp/). This is a web channel experience to search, browse, and consume SAP Best Practices and will replace the SAP Service Marketplace.

Note:

On the screen in the figure, SAP Best Practices Explorer, you can see there is a message when following the link to the SAP Best Practices Explorer suggesting that those accessing the link should sign-in with their SAP user Id (S-USER) to gain access to the detailed accelerators. For example, this access is required to view the Configuration Guides relating to the Building Blocks.

The Best Practices packages can also be downloaded to SAP Solution Manager 7.2 within the **Solution Administration (SOLADM)** transaction.

The SAP Best Practices documentation can be downloaded from SAP Service Marketplace. You can access the content on the page https:// service.sap.com/rds and then go to the respective best practice package to download the documentation. You can access the download from here. Click the download button to download the documentation. In the SAP Service Marketplace, we have access to all the content including the fact sheets, software requirements, and additional details.

More instructions to download SAP Best Practices from the SAP Service Marketplace are available at: https://support.sap.com/content/dam/SAAP/ Sol_Pack/Misc/S4HANA%20Best%20Practices%20Content%20Tour. pdf

1.6 SAP Activate – Governance, Roles & Responsibilities

Team Structure

Team	Description
SAP Implementation Team	Provides: • Product expertise • Best practices • SAP domain knowledge and experience • Proven implementation expertise • Expert technical skills
Customer Team	Provides: • Business drivers • Implementation objectives • Management and business requirements • Current industry process knowledge • Current industry system information and interface knowledge • Overall project management

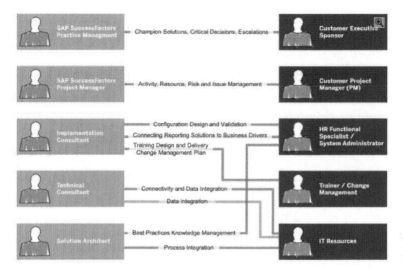

Figure 1.24 SAP Activate team structure

Image Source: SAP SE / AG

SAP Practices Management

It works closely with the *customer executive sponsor* to ensure that all the escalations are handled quickly so that there are no delays in the project.

Practice Management:

- Manages resource forecasts and staffs implementation projects
- Serves as an escalation path to assist customer executive to resolve issues

Customer Executive Sponsor

It is held accountable for the success of the project. The "Customer Executive Sponsor " does the below activities generally:

- Signs off on contractual scope of the project
- Provides and/or approves business drivers and monitors results
- Approves change requests
- Facilitates resolution of escalated issues

SAP Implementation Team -- Project Manager

Project manager is responsible for the day to day activities of the SAP SuccessFactors implementation team. Also, a project manager:

- Is responsible for completion of SAP project deliverables and obtaining customer approvals
- Creates and manages project work schedules and status updates related to SAP resources
- Escalates project issues to the Customer Project Manager

SAP Implementation Team -- Technical Consultant

Technical and architect consultants set the technical direction and support the configuration of interfaces. This consultant:

- Connects information on external data sources to solutions in the SAP SuccessFactors tools
- Liaises with customer IT to troubleshoot technical issues

SAP Team -- Implementation Consultant

Implementation consultants are assigned configuration and knowledge transfer tasks responsible for configuration. An implementation consultant:

- Facilitates decision-making through demonstration of SAP Best Practices content
- Provides configuration quality assurance though support of testing processes
- Creates defect tickets as needed
- Positions reporting solutions to support business drivers

SAP Implementation Team -- Solutions Architect

The Solutions Architect has a key role and manages:

- Data Integration
- Process Integration

Customer Project Manager

The customer project manager is managing the day to day activities of all the customer resources and reporting back to the executive sponsor on progress and issues. A customer project manager:

- Manages project plan documents and signoffs
- Manages scope and internal resource availability
- Integrates project work with other internal initiatives

Customer Functional Specialist / System Administrator

The Customer Functional Specialist / System administrators are ensuring that the configuration of the solution is meeting the business processes and the migrated data is correct. A Customer Functional Specialist / System Administrator:

- Provides description of business process
- Incrementally learns and tests configuration
- Updates and completes configuration workbooks

Customer Trainer / Change Management

The training and change management resource ensure that the users are well trained and the entire business organization is aware of the changes in business processes. This resource:

- Develops subject matter expertise via Train-the-Trainer
- Manages distribution of knowledge to the larger organization
- Manages Change Management and Communications.

Customer Team – IT Resources

And finally, the IT resources ensure that the migrated data is being prepared properly and interfaces are configured correctly. An IT resource:

- Provides details on data sources
- Manages access delivery
- Manages data delivery

Real-life case study example

Leveraging its experience gained over various engagements and industry best practices, SAP Practice Management team is proposing the following well-structured governance model that will ensure effective project level governance and delivery. The three-tier governance structure will define, delegate, monitor and guide all aspects of the engagement and focus on the following dimensions:

- Periodic performance review
- Risk and issue management at appropriate level
- Escalation management
- Ensuring management support to the engagement

This project management structure is based on the following three levels:

Strategic Level

- To provide strategic direction to the project

- Ensures that the project is aligned to the strategic vision of customer / business
- Creates business value and is aligned to its IT strategy.

Tactical Level

To ensure that the multiple work-streams in the project follow:

- Overall agreed program timelines
- Provide right Interface for all the work-streams to manage inter-dependencies
- Standardized processes like release management and change management
- Design and utilize common knowledge repository

Operational Level

To effectively monitor and control day to day operations .

The following section details the governance structure during implementation of the project.

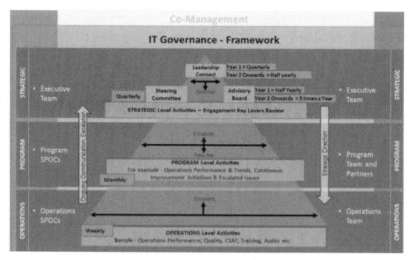

Figure 1.25 Project governance overview

Image Source: SAP SE / AG

Project Steering Committee

Key responsibilities of the Project Steering Committee are as follows:

- Monitor overall execution of the project with respect to agreed timelines
- Resolve any major issues of significant risk and impact on the project
- Review Overall Project Status Reports and take appropriate actions
- Recommend guidelines and frameworks which can be adopted for execution of project
- Oversee that assignment is carried out as per the agreed TOR and contractual conditions
- Approve changes to port share
- This committee shall oversee the implementation of the overall project,
- They will be empowered to take decisions for day-to-day activities involving the project and subsequently place the decision to Project Steering Committee for post-facto approval.

Customer Nodal Officer

There will be one Nodal Officer for each port. The key responsibilities of the Customer Nodal Officer will be as follows:

- Port Nodal Officer, who shall manage the project and ensure smooth implementation of Project.
- Port Nodal officer in consultation with the respective Business Owner will identify and nominate functional owner:
- To review deliverables submitted including SLA reports
- To carryout UAT and provide sign-off on functionality from the envisaged system
- Customer Nodal officer shall receive deliverables from Functional Owners from all departments and put forward for final sign-off from the respective Deputy Chairman.
- After receiving final ratification on deliverables recommend release of payment to Managed Service Provider by Customer
- Review and place quarterly SLA report to Dy. Chairman

- Communicate any major issues of significant risk and impact on the project at port to Project Coordinator for placing at steering committee for resolution
- Recommend guidelines and frameworks which can be adopted for execution of project at port
- Receive change requests and amendments from functional owner, review and place it to Dy Chairman for ratification.
- Participate in meetings and internal discussions for successful implementation of Project

Customer Business Owner

Head of the respective department will be Business Owner. Key responsibilities of the Business Owner

- Monitor that business targets and objectives are met by the system
- Review the critical business scenarios and results
- Review requests raised by Managed Service Provider related to BoM amendment, change requests, etc.

Customer Functional Owner

Customer Nodal officer in consultation with the respective Business Owner will identify and nominate functional owner. Key responsibilities of the Functional Owner are as follows:

- Review and integrate all test scenarios
- Ensure that business targets and objectives are met by the system
- Identify and manage critical business scenarios and validate results
- Review requests by Managed Service Provider for change request and recommend course to Business Process Owner
- Maintain standardization across the business processes
- Provide the project with indispensable technical input
- Conduct End user training and UAT
- Review deliverables submitted including SLA reports and recommend course of action to Customer Nodal Officer

IT Team

Customer Project Manager

Key responsibilities of the Customer Project Manager will be as follows:

- Project Manager shall manage the project and ensure timely engagement
- Organise project steering committee meeting
- Manages project plan documents and signoffs
- Manages scope and internal resource availability
- Integrates project work with other internal initiatives

Customer Project Co-Ordinator

Key responsibilities of the Customer Project Coordinator will be as follows:

- Project co-ordinator shall monitor the project and coordination with different locations

SAP Implementation Team Program Director

Program director will coordinate with the customer / business for any update and review. Key responsibilities will be as follows:

- Participate in the steering committee meetings
- Participate in periodic review meeting with customer and key stakeholders
- Ensure status report is send periodically to all stake holders
- Ensure that all the partners are in sync and status reported stake holders
- Conflict management, issue and dispute resolution
- Review quality of project deliverables to ensure compliance with the agreed quality measures and standards

SAP Implementation Team Project Manager

Project Manager key responsibilities will be as follows:

- Organizing, planning, directing, and coordinating the overall program effort
- Allocating resources to the project
- Conflict management, issue and dispute resolution
- Participate in all fortnightly / monthly project meetings and project review meetings

- Review quality of project deliverables to ensure compliance with the agreed quality measures and standards
- Shall ensure compliance to the terms and conditions of the contract and NDA signed with customer / business

SAP Implementation Team Project Lead

Their key responsibilities will be as follows:

- Will be at the onsite office.
- Shall be responsible for the overall contract performance and shall not serve in any other capacity under this contract.
- Shall be responsible for organizing, planning, directing, and coordinating the overall program effort.
- Shall participate in the steering committee meetings.
- Shall be responsible for overall Project Planning.
- Shall be responsible for managing the team resources and ensuring their optimum allocation.
- Shall review the integration test plan for completeness and correctness.
- Shall manage integration testing along with Solution Architect (Software) and Testing Engineers.
- Shall prepare Performance Test Plan which shall specify the business transactions that shall be tested for performance.
- Shall have extensive experience and proven expertise in managing similar multitask contracts of this type and complexity.
- Shall have a thorough understanding and knowledge of the principles and methodologies associated with program management, vendor management, quality assurance metrics and techniques, and configuration management tools.
- Shall be available onsite for full time during project implementation.

SAP Implementation Team Functional Leads

Module Leads will be designated as Functional Leads. Their key responsibilities will be as follows:

- Work with the business users of the applications and programmers to translate the business needs and requirements into functional specifications which can be used by the programmers for implementation.

- Provide guidance to customer / business on devising effective and efficient approaches to achieve the project objectives.
- Reporting status and issues to the Project Manager.
- Act as a liaison between the technology and domain.
- Assist the QA Team Leader and Testing Engineers in preparation of test plans, test cases, test data, and so on.
- Assist during User Acceptance Testing and Implementation activities.
- Review and provide guidance to Technical Writers while drafting User Manuals, Training Materials, FAQs, and so on.

Governance Schedule

- The agenda for each meeting of the Steering Committee and other committees shall be set to reflect the discussion items related to the scope of work and additional items may be added either with the agreement of the parties or at the request of either party.
- Copies of the agenda for meetings along with relevant pre-reading material shall be distributed.
- All meetings and proceedings will be documented; such documents to be distributed to both parties and copies shall be kept as a record. All actions, responsibilities, and accountabilities arising out of any meeting shall be tracked and managed.
- The parties shall ensure as far as reasonably practicable that the above formed committees shall resolve the issues and resolve the objectives placed before them and members representing that party are empowered to make relevant decisions or have easy access to empowered individuals for decisions to be made to achieve this.
- The parties will proceed in good faith so that the Steering Committee shall resolve the issues and smoothen the performance of the project.
- The parties agree to attempt to resolve all disputes arising under the Agreement, equitably and in good faith. To this end, the parties agree to provide frank, candid and timely disclosure of all relevant facts, information, and documents to facilitate the discussions between them/their representatives or senior officers.

Project Roles and Responsibilities

The Project Team consists of members from Customer / business / SAP implementation partner / team. The description of their roles and responsibilities is given in table below for real-life scenarios:

Roles	Customer / Business	SAP Implementation Team
Project Steering Committee	• Monitor overall execution of the project with respect to agreed timelines • Resolve any major issues of significant risk and impact on the project • Review Overall Project Status Reports and take appropriate actions • Recommend guidelines and frameworks which can be adopted for execution of project • Oversee that the assignment is carried out as per the agreed TOR and contractual conditions • Approve changes to port share • Approval on major decision making process	• Work with the Customer / business Steering Committee members to provide strategic directions, resolve issues, conflicts etc. • Report on engagement progress • Submit project deliverables
Project Manager	• Project Manager shall manage the project and ensure timely engagement. • Organize Project Steering Committee Meeting. • Manages project plan documents and signoffs • Manages scope and internal resource availability • Integrates project work with other internal initiatives	• Day to day management of the project • Manage overall project delivery and project scope • Establish project standards • Monitor and control project progress against work plan to ensure timely delivery • Resolve issues and escalate those that cannot be solved at the project management level to customer Project Manager

Roles	Customer / Business	SAP Implementation Team
		• Review project deliverables to enable acceptance of project deliverables
Customer Executive Sponsor	• Signs off on contractual scope of the project • Provides and/or approves business drivers and monitors results • Approves Change Requests • Facilitates resolution of escalated issues	• N/A
SAP Practices Management	• N/A	• Manages resource forecasts and staffs implementation projects • Serves as an escalation path to assist Customer Executive to resolve issues
Project Coordinator	• Project coordinator monitor the project activity on day to day basis and co-ordinate with ports and different stake holders for its smooth implementation	• N/A
Nodal Officer	• Customer Nodal Officer, who shall manage the project and ensure smooth implementation of Project. • Customer Nodal officer in consultation with the respective Business Owner will identify and nominate functional owner: • To review deliverables submitted including SLA reports • To carryout UAT and provide sign-off on functionality from the envisaged system	• N/A

Roles	Customer / Business	SAP Implementation Team
	• Customer Nodal officer shall receive deliverables from functional owners from all departments and put forward for final sign-off from the respective Deputy Chairman • After receiving final ratification on deliverables recommend release of payment to Managed Service Provider by Customer / Business	
	• Review and place quarterly SLA report to Dy. Chairman • Communicate any major issues of significant risk and impact on the project to Customer / business Project Coordinator for placing at steering committee for resolution • Recommend guidelines and frameworks which can be adopted for execution of project at port • Receive change requests and amendments from functional owner, review and place it to Dy Chairman for ratification • Participate in meetings and internal discussions for successful implementation at Port • Project schedule follow up and Functional Owners availability/ coordination during BBP sessions, training and testing, Sign off • Participate in the Milestone • Review and integrate all test scenarios and sign off	

Roles	Customer / Business	SAP Implementation Team
Business Owner	• Approve the SAP solution for their respective business area • Monitor that business targets and objectives are met by the system • Review the critical business scenarios and results • Review requests raised by Managed Service Provider related to BoM amendment, change requests, and so on • Review and monitor deliverables of Functional Owners	• N/A
Functional Owner	• Review and integrate all test scenarios • Ensure that business targets and objectives are met by the system • Identify and manage critical business scenarios and validate results • Review requests by Managed Service Provider for change request and recommend course to Business Process Owner • Maintain standardization across the business processes • Provide the project with indispensable technical input • Conduct End user training and UAT • Review deliverables submitted including SLA reports and recommend course of action to Customer Nodal Officer	• To provide guidance and training • To involve key users during BP, UAT and Training

Roles	Customer / Business	SAP Implementation Team
Functional Lead	• N/A	• Functional teams will focus on the business requirements of the respective modules • Develop documentation templates for consistency and completeness in information/data capture • Facilitate workshops for data gathering and To-Be validation • Analyze existing issues, their fundamental causes and impacts • Develop To-Be process maps • Establish the 'To-Be' EBS environment for the various Applications of modules
Technical Team	• Customer to assign a dedicated resource from IT team to work with SAP ABAP consultants	• SAP Implementation team to assign dedicated and skilled resources to project implementation to cater the development requirements via ABAP objects

Roles	Customer / Business	SAP Implementation Team
		• SAP Implementation Team members will ensure the installation, authorization profile creation and testing, applying patches and upgrades, and so on • Create and test authorization profiles • Ensure that the system is available for the project team and ensure the necessary objects are transported from the development environment to the staging or production environment, as and when required by the project team
End Users	• To provide support to Key Users during Blueprinting, Testing, and so on. Get trained on all business process in project, and utilizing the Project System	• N/A

Guiding principles

The following are some of the guiding principles based on previous experiences of the projects which will serve as useful observations to remember while implementing SAP Implementation project:

S. No.	Observation Point		To Remember
1.	Full time and experienced team		A qualified staff and dedicated team to Project Implementation need to be considered.

S. No.	Observation Point		To Remember
2.	Cost component of the Program		The budget for the Project Program shall consider all cost components such as hardware, software, training, consulting and tools etc. as identified in bid response. Any new item identified afterwards shall be taken up a new proposal.
3.	Effective monitoring and review		Independent program review and monitoring mechanism shall be set up to get direct feedback to customer / business.
4.	Learn from others		Customer / business can learn from and understand best practices from similar institutions to get more visibility on similar implementations.
5.	Managing large scale IT Program		Dividing and prioritizing the whole program into series of small programs/ systems would facilitate better management, control and visualize quick wins. It will also provide attention to business priorities.
6.	Change Management aspects		A dedicated team for Organization Change Management would be essential to manage human aspects such as resistance, unwillingness, and so on.
7.	Selection of integrated systems		Selecting a pre-integrated system, manufactured by one vendor would provide advantage in reducing technical problems.
8.	Encourage minimum change		Less customization is recommended taking into account project future version upgrade(s).
9.	Business leadership		The Program has to be run by a business leader instead of technology leader to provide importance to business.

1.7 SAP Activate, ASAP and SAP Launch – Comparison

Parameter	Old	Replaced with / New	Main improvements
New Implementation	ASAP 8.0	SAP Activate methodology for On Premise edition	- Agile Project delivery, iterative & incremental - Use of SAP best practices - Reduced Project life cycle
New Implementation	SAP Launch	SAP Activate methodology for cloud edition	- SAP BluePrint activities replaced with solution fit/gap workshops - Guided configuration
System Conversion & Landscape transformation	-	SAP Activate methodology for System Conversion / Landscape transformation (planned)	- Upto 10 key deliverables per phase and easier access to accelerators and key guides

SAP Activate methodology is effectively designed to succeed all variants of ASAP8 methodology and SAP Launch.

The SAP ecosystem is familiar with the ASAP methodology; there are some differences between SAP Activate and ASAP that you should be aware of, for an on-premise implementation:

In SAP Activate methodology we are leveraging the SAP Best Practices as a default way to build the baseline system for fit/gap.

The core project phases are reduced to four (from five in ASAP). In SAP Activate we do not have separate phases for the final preparation and go-live support, but instead execute them in one phase called *DEPLOY*.

In the SAP Jam space where you can learn about SAP Activate we describe no more than 10 key deliverables per phase. This helps those accessing the SAP Activate materials to review content and to understand the key goals of a phase.

The blueprint activities that were represented in ASAP, have been replaced with Fit/Gap analysis workshops. The project team uses the SAP Best Practices based system to validate the customer's requirement against a working baseline solution. Then the team captures the delta requirements, gaps in the backlog. This information is then used for implementation of requirements during the *Realize* phase.

1.8 SAP Activate Methodology – Quality Built-In

The 10 quality principles are based on four distinct characteristics. These are:

1. You need to understand how can you effectively implement the principles.

2. Best Practices explaining how you can best manage the area covered by this principle.

3. The typical pitfalls that customers have experienced regarding this principle and that you may not be aware of.

4. Examples of the success factors that SAP customers who have won SAP Quality Awards have identified to achieve excellence in their implementation approach.

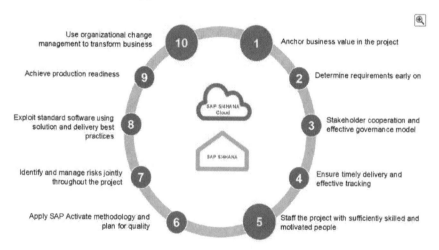

Figure 1.26 SAP Activate 10 quality principles overview

Image Source: SAP SE / AG

The preceding figure illustrates the 10 quality principles.

1. Anchor business value firmly in your project

   All involved parties must fully understand the project's strategic importance, its business objectives, and its key success criteria. These aspects should be tracked throughout the project and after going live with the software to make sure the solution meets the business requirements. This tracking also helps determine whether changes proposed to the project scope are justified by the business value they may add.

2. Staff the project with sufficiently skilled, motivated people

   Carefully recruit your project staff and select a partner who will provide you with the right mix of skills and experience. They must understand the technical and functional context in which they are working. Skills and competencies should be reviewed regularly as should people's motivation, commitment, and time allocation.

3. Use organizational change management to transform business

   Change management has to be started at the beginning of the project to ensure adoption of a business solution. Carefully select the training and communication strategies that prepare users to embrace new ways of working.

   To help achieve success on your implementation, please follow the 10 quality principles. Achieving extraordinary business transformation through the implementation of enterprise software solutions isn't a matter of luck. It requires thorough planning and commitment to succeed!

Organizations with successful SAP implementation projects can apply for SAP Quality Award. To apply, go to http://go.sap.com/corporate/en/company/quality/awards.html

Quality Built-In – SAP Activate Project Quality

SAP places quality at the centre of projects that we deliver for our Customers.

A Quality Gate provides oversight and early visibility into potential risks and issues. It has a profound impact in reducing project risk and driving customer value.

Project Quality Gate Process supports this:

- The Quality Gate Process is a formal way of specifying and recording the transition between critical stages in the project lifecycle
- Each Project Quality Gate verifies that acceptance is met for the deliverables required and actions to be completed for the associated critical stage
- The Project Quality Gate Plan is defined in the Project Management Plan

Quality Gates are built into the standard methodology. SAP places quality at the centre of the project delivery.

Quality Gates Objectives

- Assure quality at the milestones of the project
- Assure that all key deliverables and actions have been completed in compliance with the best practices
- Avoid customer dissatisfaction
- Enable project managers to continuously communicate and build quality into the project.

Quality Gates Benefits

- Enhance project quality
- Minimize project risk exposure
- Manage expectations and monitor customer satisfaction
- Improve transparency of the project
- Reduce cycle time – get it done the first time

Four Mandatory Project Quality Gates

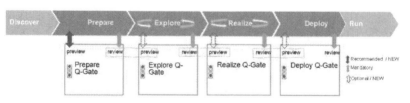

Figure 1.27 SAP Activate 4 quality gates overview

Image Source: SAP SE / AG

A minimum of four Quality Gates will be mandated to perform for SAP implementation project:

- Within complex projects with open risks that are critical, additional Q-Gates may be executed
- Within Agile projects G-Gate reviews for each release/sprint may be sufficient

Preview at begining of Prep Phase mandatory

- Quality Gates carried out at an early time can influence the phase and project results positive
- Coach and advice PM on upcoming project phase (PM standards, deliverables, customer duties, and so on.)

Review

- Check that necessary standards and project approach have been established.

Review of phase can be combined with Preview of upcoming phase

No additional effort expected – time split between Preview and Review

As stated earlier, SAP Activate has one Quality Gate in each phase. SAP Methodology provides a structured template with questions and evaluation guidance that helps teams prepare for and execute the Quality Gates.

1.9 Glossary

Configuration Guides Configuration Guides contain step by step instructions on how to configure the best practices.

Configuration Workbooks Configuration Workbooks have been completed with the Best Practices configuration settings.

Customer Team Enablement Workstream Covers the enablement of the customer project team to work on the project effectively. This includes the standard product orientation to prepare the customer for product requirements and design discussion, as well as key user and admin training to prepare the customer for test case development and test execution.

Cutover Management Workstream Covers planning and execution of activities to cutover the application into production, including the hyper-care support period shortly after cutover.

Data Migration Workstream Covers the discovery, planning, and execution of moving data to the new application.

Deliverable   A Deliverable is an outcome that is delivered during the course of the project. Several deliverables are included within a work stream.

Demonstration Scripts   Demonstration scripts and demonstration tenants can be used during the Explore Phase to identify additional configuration that is needed beyond the Best Practices content.

Enhancement Management Workstream   It covers the processes to request SAP Ariba product development changes.

Go Live   The implementation roadmap consists of one or more Go Lives. Each Go Live may correspond to the productive use of a new SAP Ariba module, an extension of functionality of an existing module, or a rollout of functionality to additional countries, departments, and so on.

There are five levels in the SAP Activate Methodology. The highest level is the Implementation Roadmap which consists of one or more Go Lives. A Go Live is broken into phases.

- Workstreams usually are associated with one phase but may start or end before or after the start of the phase. Workstreams comprise a group of deliverables.

- Deliverables are usually tangible and can be clearly verified as to whether the deliverable is complete or not. To achieve deliverables, team members work on tasks to complete the deliverable.

- Tasks should have finite start and end dates and be short in duration to ensure status of the task can be readily determined.

Implementation Roadmap   The highest level of the SAP Activate methodology is the implementation roadmap and consists of one or more Go Lives.

Integration Preparation Workstream   Covers identification of integration requirements, integration points, integration approach, and integration solution design.

Integration Setup Workstream   Covers the setup of the integration environment and middleware between the solution and any external systems.

Phase(s)   Phases are stages of the project. At the end of each phase, a quality gate exists to verify the completion of the deliverables.

Project Preparation Workstream During this workstream, the Development / Test tenant is secured. Best Practice content is installed or configured in Development or Test tenant.

Project Management Workstream Covers planning, scheduling, and governance controlling and monitoring the execution of the project.

Quality Gate A Quality Gate ensures that all the stakeholders agree that the activities of the phase have been completed and the project can go onto the next phase. Stakeholders include the members of the implementation team as well as steering committee members. A Quality Gate occurs at the end of each phase.

Sample Procurement Forms Sample procurement forms are provided so that the testing process can be accelerated.

Sample Test Data Sample test data is provided so that the testing process can be accelerated.

Solution Adoption Workstream Covers value management, organization change management, and user training.

Solution Configuration Workstream Covers the configuration and unit testing of the system to fulfill the solution design. Items that can be configured include, but not limited to, forms, workflows, user permission/ security, screen layout, reports, master data setup, notifications, and so on.

Solution Design Workstream Covers the validation of scope, identification of detailed business process requirements, fit-gap analysis, positioning of best practices, and functional design of the solution.

Solution Testing Workstream Covers test strategy, planning, test case development, and execution of User Acceptance Test, Integration Test, Performance Test, and/or System Test.

Solution Walkthrough Workstream Covers the demonstration of the configured/developed solution to the customer project team after each iteration cycle for customer acceptance and identification of adjustments needed for the next iteration.

Support Readiness Workstream Covers the establishment and setting up of the helpdesk process, incident management process, post go-live change management process, and user related operations standards and process.

Task A task is work to be performed. One or several tasks comprise a deliverable.

Workstream A workstream is a collection of related deliverables that show time relationships within a project and among other streams. Streams can span phases and are not necessarily dependent on phase starts and end.

Workstreams usually are associated with one phase but may start or end before or after the start of the phase. Chapter 2 – SAP Activate Methodology – Content Access

1.10 Access SAP Activate via SAP JAM

Working with SAP, we may have accessed Jam for various information or collaboration groups. The SAP Activate Methodology Jam site was opened in July 2015 for everybody to access. In 2015 we had about 3000 users, at the end of 2016 there were over 14,000 registered users. This JAM site acts like a co-operation environment for people to work and talk about the methodology, understand usage, its application in their projects and ask questions that are relevant for the issue that they are dealing with.

The solution specific roadmap content for the implementations are best located in the SAP S/4HANA roadmaps available in the SAP Roadmap Viewer.

Please find enclosed the links to the two sub-group sites available on the SAP Methodologies JAM site. One is for Cloud and the other is for on-premise solutions.

a. **SAP Activate methodology for Cloud**

   https://jam4.sapjam.com/groups/about_page/4IpPKa7JY
   lAQQnA0mmHXcb

b. **SAP Activate methodology for on-premise solutions**

   https://jam4.sapjam.com/auth/company_selector/EAENVgSP
   Sqyji1kDQjWt8H

Figure 1.28 SAP methodologies overview

Image Source: SAP SE / AG

When we enter the Jam site there are a couple of things to understand:

1. To enter the Jam site we need to register through the link provided in the figure.
2. The site is structured to allow us to access 'accelerator'; files (for example, template, example document, and guide) that will help us accomplish the activity.
3. To make it easier to navigate, we cover deliverables under a *Key Deliverable* structure within a phase.

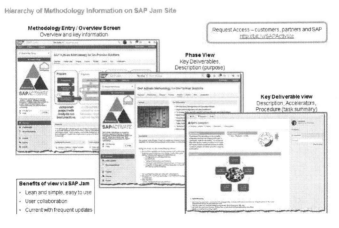

Figure 1.29 Hierarchy of methodology information on SAP Jam site

Image Source: SAP SE / AG

The entry screen is an overview page with a few items that will be found in each of the sub-group sites (Cloud, on-premise).

There is a featured content panel where we highlight the key items, for example, the WBS template for the new implementation project, or a link to the roadmap viewer to access the roadmaps.

Collaboration is available in this environment; the site always shows the latest questions and a link to resources.

Methodology in SAP Jam – Phase view

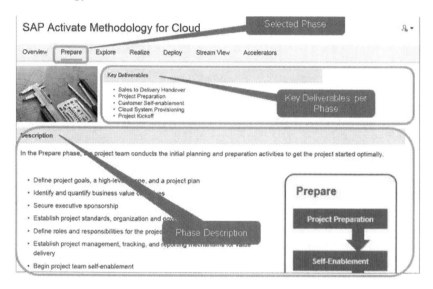

Figure 1.30 Methodology in SAP Jam phase wise view

Image Source: SAP SE / AG

1.11 Access SAP Activate via Roadmap Viewer

The SAP Roadmap Viewer can be found at https://go.sap.corp/ roadmapviewer or from a link on the SAP Methodologies JAM page. Here you will find the detailed roadmaps and accelerators summarized on the SAP Methodologies JAM site.

The roadmap viewer can be accessed from SAP methodologies Jam Site and SAP Solution Manager.

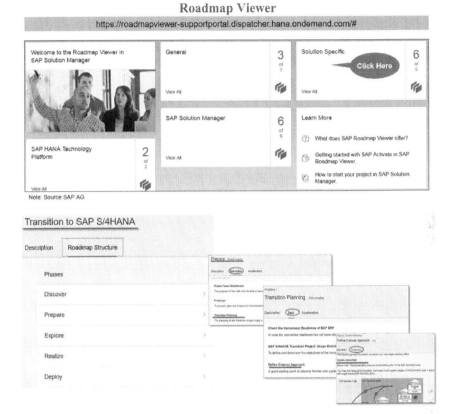

Figure 1.31 Roadmap viewer overview

Image Source: SAP SE / AG

Roadmap viewer is a tool that gives access to a full work breakdown structure of a particular project type. The content is available in an on-line Fiori based environment.

It is hosted or managed within the ATP HANA Cloud platform. It shows the SAP Activate roadmaps for SAP S/4HANA and the SAP Activate roadmaps for other solutions.

We call them general WBSs, which are applied to different On-Premise solutions or Cloud solutions. The hierarchy that we see in this environment (unlike the SAP JAM sites) is the standard core WBS hierarchy of the WBS of:

- Phase
- Deliverable
- Tasks
- With an additional view by workstream

Key features:

- Roadmap Viewer allows customers and partners to view Solution Manager Roadmaps online
- Roadmap Viewer runs on the SAP S/4HANA Cloud Platform

Initially the Roadmap Viewer will show:

- SAP S/4HANA Roadmaps
- SAP Activate Methodology Roadmaps
- Other Solution Manager Roadmaps

Each Roadmap is a three level hierarchy based on the SAP Activate methodology:

- Level 1: Phases
- Level 2: Deliverables
- Level 3: Tasks

It provides description of each phase, deliverable, and task and links to related accelerators:

- SAP S/4HANA release specific content
- Relevant SAP Activate accelerators

Navigation via phase is done by selecting a specific phase (for example, PREPARE, EXPLORE, REALIZE, and DEPLOY) as seen in the screenshot on the left-hand side of the figure, Roadmap Viewer Navigation (by Phase or Workstream).

Navigation through workstreams is done by selecting a specific workstream; this then lists all the deliverables in that particular workstream.

Click a deliverable to see the following:

- Description
- Tasks
- Accelerators

Click an Accelerator to display/download content that is relevant for the selected deliverable.

Click a Task to see the full available task description (you may also find additional accelerators).

Published SAP S/4HANA and SAP Activate Roadmaps

General Methodologies - SAP Activate

- SAP Activate Methodology for New Cloud Implementations (Public Cloud)
- SAP Activate Methodology for Business Suite and On-Premise - Agile
- SAP Activate Methodology for Business Suite and On-Premise - Waterfall

SAP S/4 HANA

- Transition to SAP S/4 HANA
- SAP Activate: Implement and Configure SAP S/4 HANA Marketing Cloud
- SAP Activate: Implement and Configure SAP S/4 HANA Professional Services Cloud
- SAP Activate: Implement and Configure SAP S/4 HANA Enterprise Management Cloud
- SAP Activate: Implement and Configure SAP S/4 HANA Finance Cloud

Check into the Roadmap Viewer regularly because new or updated roadmaps are frequently published.

When downloading a roadmap from the SAP Roadmap viewer you receive a ZIP file with three different files/formats:

- Spreadsheet
- File to load to Microsoft Project
- File to load to SAP Solution manager as a project

Roadmap Viewer Navigation (by Phase or Workstream)

Roadmap Viewer Navigation (by Phase or Workstream)

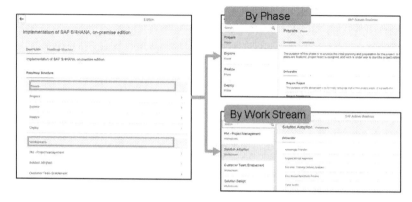

Both options will list related deliverables

Figure 1.32 Roadmap viewer navigation (by phase or by workstream)

Image Source: SAP SE / AG

You may navigate through the roadmap either using:

- Project phases
- Project workstreams

Both options will list, related deliverables.

Navigating via phase is done through selecting a specific phase (for example, Prepare, Explore, Realize, and Deploy).

Navigation through workstreams is done by selecting a specific workstream; this then lists all the deliverables in that particular workstream.

The representation on the screen portrays the same when navigating *by phase* or *by workstream*; we see a list of deliverables.

1.12 Access SAP Activate via SAP Solution Manager

For Project Management there are three tiles which are offered by SAP:

a. My Projects

b. My Task

c. Project Analytics

For transaction support see:

http://help.sap.com/solutionmanager72

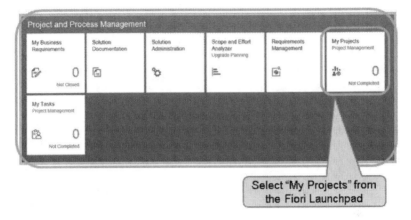

Figure 1.33 *My Projects navigation from Fiori launchpad*
Image Source: SAP SE / AG

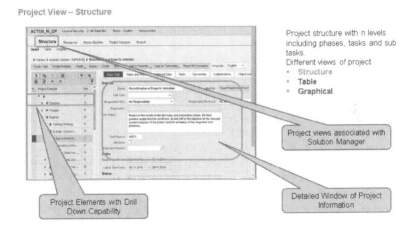

Figure 1.34 *Overview of project view structure*
Image Source: SAP SE / AG

Table views associated with Solution Manager are structured in a tabular format for increased user experience.

Project elements with Drill down capability can be selected to display specific project artifacts.

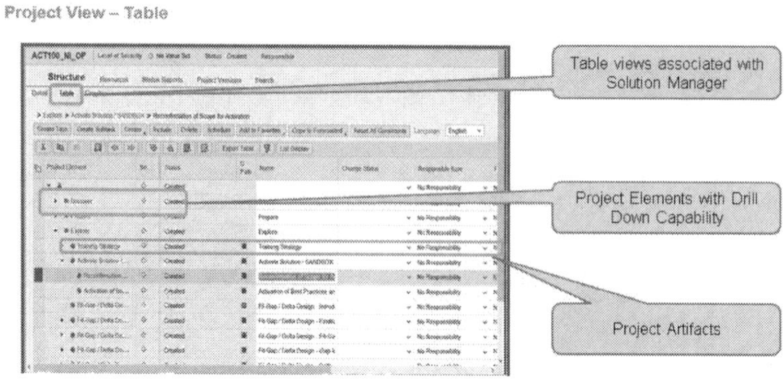

Project View – Table

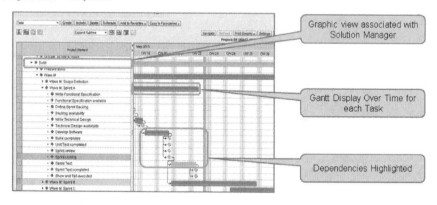

Figure 1.35 Overview of project view table
Image Source: SAP SE / AG

Within the graphical view, you can add, remove, and modify project elements.

Gantt Display over time for each task.

Dependencies are highlighted for specific project elements.

Project View – Graphical

Figure 1.36 Overview of project view graphical
Image Source: SAP SE / AG

By selecting the project analytics window, you can display the detailed Project and Schedule Information.

Each pane can be selected to display the specific task information.

NOTES

NOTES

NOTES

NOTES

NOTES

NOTES

CHAPTER 2

Journey New Implementation (In Cloud)

Let us now look at the choice of deployment strategy in SAP S/4HANA Cloud, on-premise, or in a hybrid solution.

There are differences and benefits in each of these deployment strategies. This explains our actions and whether there is a possibility for finding the right balance between efficiency, speed of updates, flexibility in control in the on-premise environment, the efficiency that we get in the Cloud, as well as the speed of updates in the Cloud.

A number of businesses are shifting their solution thinking from always being in on-premise (hosting their own environment in their data centers and using their own IT organization) to thinking about the environment more strategically and assessing the ability to move some of their solution functionality into the Cloud.

The move to Cloud solutions has accelerated and SAP can support both the on-premise and Cloud deployments of SAP S/4HANA.

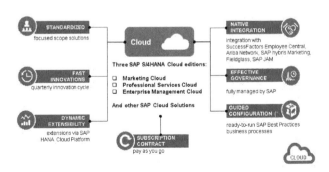

Figure 2.1 SAP S/4HANA cloud solutions

Image source – SAP AG / SE

In this unit we focus on SAP S/4HANA Cloud, however the general approach and difference from on-premise implementations are applicable to other SAP Cloud solutions.

Some key points that need to be considered in order to understand the approach to Cloud implementations. These points are as follows:

a. Innovation

b. Roles

c. System landscape

d. Handover to support

e. Project timelines.

SAP ACTIVATE for new implementations of SAP Cloud Solutions

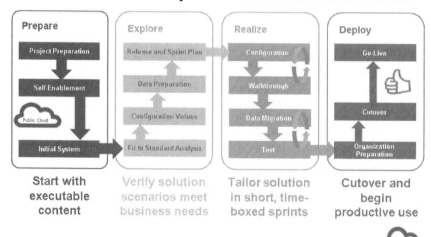

Figure 2.2 SAP ACTIVATE for new implementations of SAP cloud solutions
Image source – SAP AG / SE

This simple high-level summary view looks similar to other SAP Activate journeys. This view is for a new implementation of SAP S/4HANA Cloud editions.

The Prepare phase has similarities to an on-premise implementation, where we set up and launch a project. The difference in the Cloud implementation is that in the Prepare phase, the project team does some initial solution enablement with the customer. Later they leave the customer with materials to review as self-enablement. We start up the initial system in the Prepare phase ready for *Fit to Standard Analysis*.

With Cloud systems we have standard system processes; the systems allow for tailoring, however, requirements outside of the standard scope may require solutions external to the system. In the Explore phase we perform *Fit to Standard* functionality that we have in the Cloud solution. We also try to understand the configuration values that need to be set up in the system; that includes adjusting the organizational structures and Chart of Accounts. In this phase we also get the data ready for data load.

Standardized solutions have limited ability to close system gaps within the system. We configure the cloud solution at the start of the Realize phase in short implementation cycles using the tailoring/configuration tool of that solution followed by a walkthrough with the customer team. For SAP S/4HANA Cloud there is the *Guided Configuration* tool; for C4C there is an IMG-like structure, for SuccessFactors spreadsheets are uploaded with table content. Data migration and end-to-end testing completes the phase.

The high-level Deploy phase is relatively standard for all the journeys. Here we check the organizational readiness to perform the Cutover followed by a period of post go-live support. We may do Cutover simulations in more complex cases. In Simple Cloud solutions, it is a straightforward Cutover activity.

We begin using the *Starter System* at the end of the Prepare phase or very early in the Explore phase. We need to have the Starter System in place for *Fit to Standard* workshops.

The note (*) that the Starter System is removed and replaced by the *P-System* (the production system) during the Realize phase means that the environment changes as we go through the later stages of the Realize phase. When we start up the Production System, the Starter System is repurposed for the P-System and the customer will go-live in that P-System.

This is different from the traditional on-premise implementations where we keep the entire transport system in place and have all the items and systems in the landscape up and running throughout the entire project and then into operations.

Additional notes describe some of the system-related activities per phase.

Key Deliverables per Phase

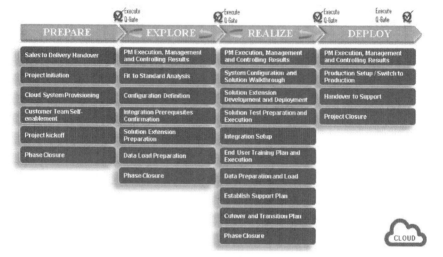

Figure 2.3 SAP ACTIVATE key deliverables per phase

Image Source: SAP SE / AG

2.1 Prepare Phase

In the Prepare Phase, the project team conducts the initial planning and preparation activities to get the project started optimally.

The phase activities are as follows:

a. Define project goals, a high-level scope, and a project plan

b. Identify and quantify business value objectives

c. Secure executive sponsorship

d. Establish project standards, organization and governance

e. Define roles and responsibilities for the project team

f. Establish project management, tracking and reporting mechanisms for value delivery

g. Begin customer team self-enablement

h. Prepare the project environment

i. Download the business process overviews and documents

j. Project team orientation

k. Gain access to the cloud system

The purpose of the Project Kick-off deliverable is to kick-off the Project and ensure that all the needed information is shared with the resources for a successful project execution.

Key deliverables

a. Project Charter

b. Project Management Plan including Governance

c. Project Schedule

d. Project Budget

Accelerators

a. **Work Breakdown Structure (WBS)**

b. WBS Stream view

c. Project Management Plan

d. Risk Management

e. Project Logistics Template

f. Project setup Checklist

g. Issues Tracking Template

h. Change Request Tracking Template

i. Solution specific Accelerators (Reference – JAM site).

2.2 Explore Phase

In the Explore phase, the project team reviews the solution scenarios to verify that business requirements can be met within the boundaries of the solution and project scope. During this process, configuration values are identified and added to sprint backlog list for use in the Realize phase. A preconfigured solution with customer specific scope is used to facilitate this phase.

The phase activities are as follow:

a. Prepare and conduct solution validation workshops

b. Confirm solution fit to required business processes

c. Continue with customer team enablement

    d. Identify master data and organizational setup requirements

    e. Identify and define configuration values

    f. Review data requirements and begin data cleansing

    g. Prepare for integration to legacy system as required

Key deliverables

    a. Project Management Plan(s)

    b. Risk & issue log(s)

    c. Configuration Definition

    d. User Access & Security

    e. Extension Specification

    f. Network Connectivity Checks

    g. Security Checks

    h. Adaptation Specification

    i. Data Migration Plan

    j. Specifications for migration programs

    k. Sign-Off documentation

Accelerators

    a. Agile and Scrum meeting guideline (s)

    b. Agile and Change Request Template (s)

    c. Project quality gate scorecard

    d. Status template

    e. Open issues template

    f. Solution specific accelerators (Reference – JAM site).

    g. Product /Sprint backlog template

    h. Extension field specification

    i. Data migration plan

    j. Data load planning template

    k. Data design

    l. Data definition

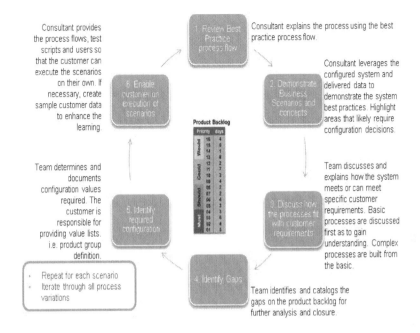

Figure 2.4 Fit to standard - workshop approach
Image Source: SAP AG / SE

Let us look at the gap identification and delta design.

Once a gap is identified, we go through the delta design activities to decide the process of covering that gap.

If it is going to be an update of the existing processes, we need to decide if we have the ability to expand the process and adjust UI or look for changes to the standard functionality without affecting the solution's ability to be updated.

If the consultants or experts decide that we may need an extension, this capability will be developed outside of the system.

There are a few decisions taken by the team as they go through the delta design activities. This leads to release and sprint planning. In Cloud implementations, we will have one release, rather than multiple releases.

As the scope and the number of Cloud modifications is going to be minimal, we may not need to modify the standard release plans unless we are dealing with a sizable implementation of the enterprise edition. For this, we may have multiple ways of releasing the capabilities incrementally, starting with the baseline functionality and then expanding into the advanced cases that are not as critical for the business.

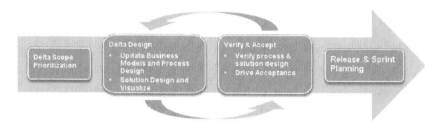

Figure 2.5 EXPLORE phase > Gap identification / Delta design

Image Source: SAP SE / AG

2.3 Realize Phase

In the Realize phase, the project team uses series of iterations to incrementally build and test a complete business and system environment that is based on the business scenarios and process requirements.

The key Realize phase activities are outlined as follows:

a. Configure the solution in the quality environment using incremental built in time-boxed iterations and the sprint backlog list

b. Continue with project team enablement on key concepts and system administration

c. Walk through solution processes with stakeholders

d. Execute data migration

e. Integrate to legacy systems as required

f. Conduct overall end-to-end testing of the solution

g. Create Cutover plan

h. Prepare for change management and end user training

For SAP S/4HANA Cloud we can use the guided configuration screens.

Therefore, it is a set of self-service configuration UIs that simplify the way that the system is configured. They are like a layer that is sitting above configuration transactions and tables.

We can do adjustments of the standard organizational structure delivered by adjusting Master data, adjusting additional settings like distribution channel source, Sales Organization and Purchasing Organizations. This helps us to set up the configuration in the system.

We access the Self Service Configuration for SAP S/4HANA Cloud / configuration transaction by going into the configuration UI. There we review the values, adjust the values, and save them. The usage of this environment is dynamic. It is similar to the usage of IMG configuration tables. This deals with the specific areas and configuration settings, which are simpler compared to the traditional setting.

For example, if we are going to configure a process within the standard On-Premise solution in the IMG, we may need to adjust multiple tables to reflect the configuration in this self-service configuration UI. If we want to make changes that impact multiple small organizational areas, we can do that much faster in the self-service configuration UIs.

We emphasize the need for the team to undertake solution walkthroughs in the Realize phase. It is important that the project team engages the business users and shows them the solution being built, so that we can iterate the build and validation of the solution (in an Agile like approach).

Even though we may not be using a full-blown scrum for iterations, with a rigid sprint structure, we do have a requirement for the project team to do the solution walk-through. Therefore, after they configure the functionality, they show the customer that aspect of the working solution and solicit feedback. Based on that feedback, they may need to do additional adjustments.

We will see that there are standard pre-delivered scripts and pre-delivered test plans for testing the SAP S/4HANA Cloud solution.

These tests are run automatically in the background. It comes pre-delivered with the solution as part of the best practices and we will be able to evaluate and review the results. The testing functionality gives the details of each step that is being executed. It shows the items that succeeded or failed and each screen is captured. We can always go back and look at the detailed test results, or if applicable where an error/defect occurred.

The next figure looks at the wider testing of the solution; if defects occur there then the configuration is fixed and tested again with the delivered test before returning to the full solution test.

Key deliverables

   a. Project Management Plan(s)

b. Risk & Issue log(s)

c. Knowledge transfer

d. Solution configuration

e. Solution documentation

g. Forms enablement

h. Reports

i. Solution walkthrough

j. Solution extension development

k. Solution extension deployment on production

l. Integration setup in the Test / Q System / Production

m. Solution test preparation

n. Test plans

o. Solution test execution report

p. Data load test results

q. Defect resolution

r. Data quality assessment

s. **End User (EU)** training plan

t. (EU) training

u. Change management plan

v. Value audits

w. Technical operations and handover plan

x. Cut-over plan

y. Production system setup

z. Sign-Off documentation

Accelerators

a. Agile Scrum meeting guidelines

b. Agile and Change Request Templates

c. Project Quality Gate Scorecard

d. Status Template

e. Open Issues Template

f. SAP Help documentation

g. Guided Configuration

h. Testing Scenario Template

i. Agile Testing approach

j. Solution specific Accelerators (Reference – JAM site)

k. Data load planning Template

l. SAP help documentation

m. Learning room (logon required)

n. Cutover strategy

o. Cutover Plan Templates

p. Data Load planning Templates

q. Quality Gate Checklist

2.4 Deploy Phase

The project team prepares the system for production release in the Deploy phase. It switches to the production environment and conducts sustainment activities post go-live.

The key Deploy phase activities are as follows:

a. Execute the cutover plan

b. Business operations transformation to the new system

c. Transfer from implementation support to production support

d. Close the project

Key deliverables

a. Project Management Plan(s)

b. Risk & Issue log(s)

c. Customer Solution Live in the cloud

d. Data migration load validated

e. Solution accepted (sign-Off)

f. Sign-Off documentation

Accelerators

a. Agile SCRUM meeting guidelines

b. Agile and Change Request Templates

c. Project Quality Gate scorecard

d. Status Template

e. Open Issues Template

f. Cutover Plan documents

g. Quality gate Checklist

h. Quality gate scorecard template

i. Solution specific Accelerators (Reference – JAM site)

2.5 Additional Information

Explain how the SAP Activate methodology guides teams implementing solutions in the public cloud?

This figure is another high-level summary representation of the new implementation of SAP S/4HANA Cloud. In addition this figure shows systems involved across the phase timeline; this shows transitioning from the Starter System into the Q-System and then into the Production System.

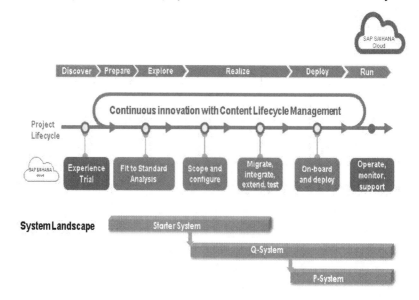

Figure 2.6 Explain how the SAP Activate methodology guides teams implementing solutions in the public cloud

Image Source: SAP AG / SE

NOTES

NOTES

NOTES

NOTES

NOTES

NOTES

NOTES

Chapter 3

Journey New Implementation (On-Premise)

Explain the key deliverables per phase of S/4 HANA Activate methodology (On-Premise)?

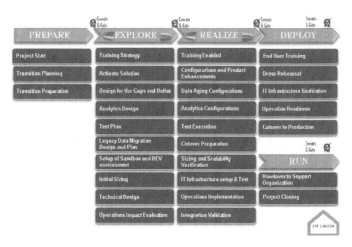

Figure 3.1 Key deliverables per phase of S/4 HANA Activate methodology (On-Premise)

Image source – SAP AG / SE

3.1 Prepare Phase

The project is initiated. Results from Discover phase needs to be considered.

Key deliverables

a. Initiation

b. Planning

c. Team enablement

  d. Organizational change management

  e. Transition planning

  f. Transition preparation

3.2 Explore Phase

Validation of the solution delivered to the customer based on the standard process documentation is its main purpose. In the Fit-Gap analysis the configuration for each business priority is determined and designs for the configuration are reviewed. In all work steams executable plans in high details are developed. The development landscape is set up, a technical design is developed. Operation impact is evaluated.

There are several Key Deliverables in the *Application: Design & Configuration* Work stream in the EXPLORE phase.

Based on the best practices we have the sandbox environment. It is fully activated and ready to go but we may not want to use this environment '*as-is*' in our Fit/Gap workshops. The '*as-is*', with standard best practice content (organizational structure, master data), may not fit in every single customer situation. To remedy this, we create a customer-specific Baseline Build. In this activity, we are adjusting that sandbox system and building the character features that we want to show during the Fit/Gap Analysis. We will adjust the baseline for the customer in those areas in scope for the Fit/Gap Analysis '*Workshop A*'.

One way to create the customer-specific Baseline Build is to build the functionality in the system.

Instead of investing time in prototyping a functional solution (that we may not have a design for) we may instead prefer to visualize that functionality in a dedicated visualization tool. In addition we may mark up workshop presentation materials with how the standard screens would look for the customer with their data.

Once we have the system Baseline Build ready, we conduct the Fit/Gap Analysis; this consists of four steps.

  • We start with the Solution Validation (Workshops A) where we do the walkthroughs. We show the process flows and explain to the customer, how the system works out of the box and walk-through any additional functionality or in the sandbox environment visualization of the Baseline Build. We capture the requirements in the form of user stories in what we call a backlog. Multiple workshop A's are planned to cover full scope of the project.

- Following the Solution Validation, we will always have a Backlog Prioritization of requirements. The highest priority features are used to plan the solution Design for Gaps and Deltas (Workshops B).

- We then have the detail information required to complete Release and Sprint Planning to take into the Realize phase.

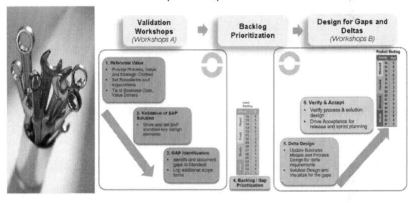

Figure 3.2 EXPLORE Phase > Application: Design & configuration considerations

Image source – SAP AG / SE

In workshop A, our objective is to do fit/gap analysis to capture the delta changes. Using MoSCoW prioritization rule, set priority of the requirements.

Then start design & build activity..

Application -- Design & Configuration Considerations

In Agile projects, we have user stories to capture the requirements. These user stories capture how the functionality should be behaving for a particular role to provide benefits.

The requirement is explained in business language instead of a technical language. The explanation includes how the requirement will be tested and the test confirmation criteria that will be used by the product owner to judge or review whether the delivered functionality fit to requirement. This is a nice approach to ensure that the product owners and the business users are not only thinking in terms of their own needs but also validating if the delivered solution meets the prioritized requirements raised by others for specific business roles.

One important thing, we need to make a note about is the level of documentation that we need to create in the project.

We need to know the volume of documentation the project team would be creating, where it will be stored and how it would be maintained and its value. The objective is to provide valuable shippable content / product features to the business, taking into account continuous improvement initiatives as part of consistent inspection, adaptation, and customer feedback loops.

This is not necessary for the project but essential for the customer. The customer's functional and technical support operations teams need to have solution information before the solution goes live.

It is required to think beyond the scope of the project and look at what level of detail is valuable and will be maintained. We should not be copying the help files or the Standard Documentation of best practices and use them as solution documentation. We can leverage the documentation without a lot of copy and paste.

We should document things like decision rationale, why certain things are configured in a certain way and explain that level of detail. The documentation should not be a series of screen shots of content - as this content can be seen using a link to the configuration content and is not easily maintained.

If the Solution Documentation is used and maintained (that is, valued) then it can be regarded as an ASSET (else it is a historical reference that can be misleading if not labelled as a historic record).

If there is a mix of Solution Documentation and links to configuration and executable objects, then we can describe this as SOLUTION INFORMATION.

So, valued Solution Information can be described as SOLUTION INFORMATION ASSETS.

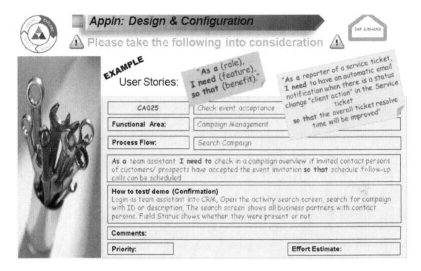

Figure 3.3: Application: Design & configuration considerations – User stories example

Image source – SAP AG / SE

Working Software is more important than documentation. But it DOES NOT mean to produce NO DOCUMENTATION at all !!!

Keep it valuable, align with the organization perspective and agree solution documentation that is valued and can be maintained.

Solution documentation that is valued and maintained is an INFORMATION ASSET for the organization.

The Solution Information Assets will be stored in SAP Solution Manager.

As we go through these workshops, we may use process-modeling tools. We recommend the usage of the BPMN modeling capabilities inside SAP Solution Manager 7.2 (SolMan) - adjusting those business process models that come with the best practices as input to the fit/gap analysis and adjusted further for the agreed design to gaps and deltas coming from the Fit workshops.

The format of the documents should take into account the latest SAP Solution Manager functionality and agreed in advance with the customer as providing Solution Information Assets.

The documents are recommended to be held in SAP Solution Manager and approved with three digital signatures representing:

- The author
- The solution provider
- The business

Prior to approval the document can be reviewed by many people.

The project can agree to deliver the Functional Specification (for developments to resolve *gaps*) and Configuration Design (to resolve *deltas*) documents as part of the Realize phase - but all key design decisions should be captured and signed off in the EXPLORE phase.

Key deliverables of Design for Gaps and Deltas

Figure 3.4: Key deliverables of design for gaps and deltas

Image source – SAP AG / SE

The Fit Gap analysis in the SAP Methodology is based on the best practices. Evaluate the fit of the process to the best practices first.

Validate the solution and collect all gaps in business processes for each business priority.

To prepare the execution prioritize the findings and validate the gaps according to their business value. From this Delta design plan is derived.

System and Data Migration for New Implementation

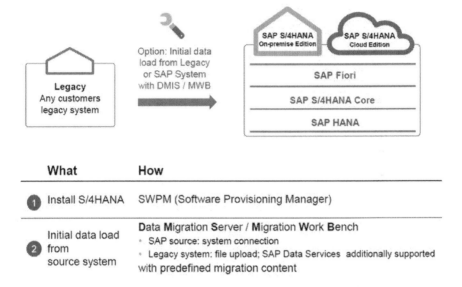

What	How
① Install S/4HANA	SWPM (Software Provisioning Manager)
② Initial data load from source system	Data Migration Server / Migration Work Bench • SAP source: system connection • Legacy system: file upload; SAP Data Services additionally supported with predefined migration content

Figure 3.5: System and data migration for new Implementation

Image source – SAP AG / SE

Additional Key deliverables

- Analytics design
- Data migration design

Testing Considerations

Customers do not expect a traditional waterfall approach where the build may take 12 months or more before bringing a solution to the business.

Requirements to be delivered in each sprint should be worked out across teams and have a functional focus for each sprint execution.

An example project build may have three months, or less, build for the first release. They then work on the next release where they plan to enhance and extend the capability.

Some Roadmaps may refer to some alternative test stage names such as: **Single Functional Test (SFT)** or **Functional Integration test (FIT)**.

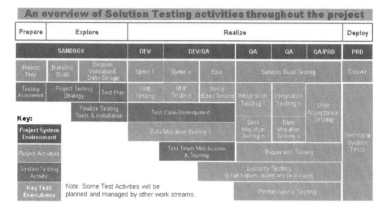

Figure 3.6 EXPLORE Phase > Testing considerations
Image source – SAP AG / SE

3.3 Realize Phase

In this phase the solution is incrementally built and tested based on the scenarios and process identified in the EXPLORE phase. Adoption activities occur and operations are planned.

Key Deliverables

Figure 3.7 Key deliverables of realize phase
Image source – SAP AG / SE

Configurations and Product Enhancements

It is a refresher of the Build Sprints and Firm-up Sprints mentioned in the earlier sessions.

The teams that build the solution take the required capabilities from the backlog, master file and start building those capabilities for an end-to-end scenario. They build and continuously test up to the Firm-up Sprint. In the Firm-up sprint the unit builds are integrated (to complete the delivery of an epic/scenario) and string tests can be delivered.

When they finalize the sprint testing, they are also in the process of building the solution documentation that is used for operations.

We do not skip the integration and user acceptance tests are at the end of the phase. It is observed in the Agile projects that these tests have fewer defects (mainly as a result of the earlier inspection points). In waterfall projects potentially following an iterative approach, we have less validation of the build and find more defects in the integration testing and UAT.

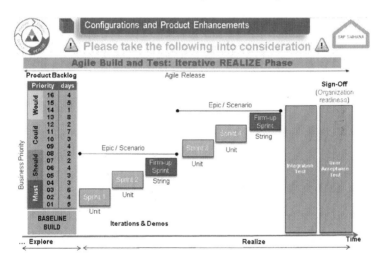

Figure 3.8 REALIZE Phase > Configurations and product enhancements

Image source – SAP AG / SE

Sprint Execution

Following an Agile approach, the *Configuration and Product Enhancements* are delivered in Sprints within a Wave – a sprint execution process is shown in the figure below.

When they are planning the sprint, they pick the user stories that are highlighted as the highest priority stories by the product owner. They bring them into the sprint and plan all the tasks and activities that need to be executed. They execute those activities in sprint realization and conduct the daily stand up SCRUM meetings. Towards the end of the sprint, they review the functionality and demo it to the owner of the user story and seek to gain acceptance for the sprint realization. At the end of a Sprint, the team will conduct a *retrospective* to consider and agree how they can improve their sprint activities.

Configuration and Product Enhancements

Figure 3.9 REALIZE Phase > Sprint execution

Image source – SAP AG / SE

Users can use many tools including the product backlog. This can be a simple spreadsheet (for example, using the product backlog template accelerator in the methodology) or use a more sophisticated backlog management tool like *VersionOne*.

The results of the sprint planning are brought on to the Scrum-board. The team uses the Scrum-board as a visible tracking mechanism and displays the sprint progress and any *blockers*.

They conduct the daily Scrum-board meetings. These daily Scrum-board meetings are conducted with the team standing looking at the Scrum-board. In this process, they have visibility of the status of the individual user stories. The team uses the backlog to create *burndown charts* to track their progress towards the goal of the Sprint.

Configuring the solution is similar to the configuration in the SAP Business Suite. It is a very similar process. We enter into the configuration activity through SAP Solution Manager - having selected an IMG configuration activity. This is not different from the implementation of SAP Business Suite but the configuration tables may be different.

Where a configuration activity is not listed in the IMG then it should be added to this structure so that it can be selected in SAP Solution Manager to configure and document the solution.

The development system should also have a setting to track changes made.

Note: Configuration of an on-premise solution is different to that of a Cloud solution.

Users can capture the solution documentation for the configuration in *Solution Manager*.

When you are using the simple documentation for Solution Configuration, you capture why those changes are made (we do not need pages of documents and historic screen shots that are not maintained by the solution or support team).

You can simply capture the configuration object links in SAP Solution Manager and a simple capture of what has changed and why.

3.4 Deploy Phase

Purpose - The purpose of the DEPLOY phase is to finalize readiness of the organization, solution and its supporting tools and processes for production Go-Live. This includes, but is not limited to, system tests, end-user training, system management, and Cutover activities (including data migration and initial support post-cutover).

There is one deliverable in the Key Deliverable *Technical and System Testing*.

We may be finalizing some of the technical system tests. These tests can also be described by some customers as part of **Operations Acceptance Testing (OAT)**.

The testing in this phase may include testing printers. It is sometimes surprising that the teams test the printers in the QA system but forget to test it in the production system. When we go-live, if the production system cannot print, this can impact our ability to execute the business processes.

The series of tests that should be executed in our production environment will be captured in the Test Strategy and agreed with the application operations team. Responsibilities for the testing may lie outside the remit of the test manager - but they should capture the test requirements and ensure that the ownership of the activity is accepted.

We need to ensure that the production environment is tested as *"ready to go-live"*.

The system performance testing may always be a separate exercise in this Deploy Phase. It is often combined with the user acceptance testing.

The important thing is that early in the project the Test Strategy is agreed and the team is clear on what testing will be performed, when it will be performed, and in which environment.

In terms of project communication, we recommend that you have *Call to Arms* meetings in the last weeks and days before Go-Live.

These meetings are short, sharp, clear and focus the team on activities that need to be done that day and vision success. This is to make sure that everybody is ready and aware of the Cutover and increasing the urgency of the remaining actions to meet the go-live timetable (and not *'drift'*). The focus from the *"Call to Arms"* meetings should mean the teams are ready to go live on time.

It is better to be prepared and have a successful go-live, than not being prepared and then dealing with the issues when go-live occurs.

The initial period of support post go-live is sometimes called *Hypercare Support*. The project team will be there to resolve and close any issues not covered by the core application support team. The project team will also undertake some workload analysis to support some analysis on the correct usage of the solution.

Project Closing

The purpose of it is to ensure that all open tasks are handed over to the support organization.

Procedure includes:

a. Finalize project closeout report

b. Obtain Sign-Off for project closure

Key Deliverables

Figure 3.10 DEPLOY Phase > Key deliverables per phase

Image source – SAP AG / SE

3.5 Additional Information

Projects adopting a waterfall approach may decide to not have sandbox or demo environment with a baseline set up, instead proposing to *start from scratch* to build a solution and not use Fit/Gap Analysis workshops.

Waterfall projects may also decide to undertake traditional process decomposition and detailed design. Following this approach can often miss taking advantage of leveraging the SAP best practices and pre-built functionality that comes with the system.

SAP recommends the usage of best practices to jumpstart the projects - not only for SAP S/4HANA implementations but for implementing all SAP on-premise solutions where we may have **Rapid Deployment solutions (RDSs)** and defined consulting solutions.

NOTES

NOTES

NOTES

NOTES

NOTES

NOTES

CHAPTER 4

Journey System Conversion for SAP S/4 HANA

Journey System Conversion for SAP S/4HANA - Key Deliverables per Phase

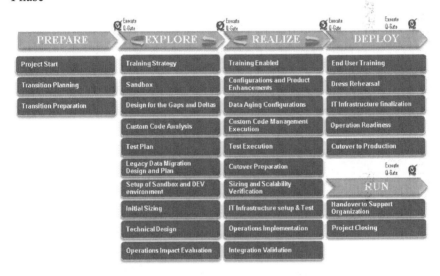

Figure 4.1 JOURNEY system conversion for SAP S/4HANA > Journey Overview > Key deliverables per phase

Image source – SAP AG / SE

System Conversion – System & Data Migration

The system conversion is not available to SAP S/4 HANA.

The figure shows some of the differences (in blue) between a Business Suite and a SAP S/4HANA environment.

Customers who want to change their current system into an SAP S/4HANA system (Database, NetWeaver and Application transition) in one step can benefit from the following:

- Migration without reimplementation
- No disruption for existing business processes
- Re-evaluation of customization and existing process flows

There are tools available to help complete these activities; **Software Update Manager (SUM)** and **Database Migration Option (DMO)** are used for rapid database migration.

	What	How
✱	Installation **and** migration	Rapid Database Migration of SAP Business Suite to SAP S/4HANA (all **one step migration**, including Finance Logistics and conversion) using SUM with DMO

Figure 4.2 System Conversion – System & data migration
Image source – SAP AG / SE

4.1 Prepare Phase

The project is initiated. The project is planned in a *Migration Planning Workshop for System Conversion*. You need to consider the results from the Discover phase as well. The Project plan can be further detailed out in the Explore phase. The Prepare phase ends with a first Quality Gate to ensure proper project preparation.

Key Deliverables

a. Project start

b. Transition planning

c. Transition preparation

d. Initiation

e. Planning

f. Team enablement

g. Organizational change management

4.2 Explore Phase

The Explore phase drives detailed planning of the technical architecture, and the conversion of SAP ERP to SAP S/4 HANA.

By the end of the EXPLORE phase, the technical and functional conversion is fully planned in detail, and ready for execution.

The assessment on custom coding from the PREPARE phase is used to develop a plan to adjust the custom coding and to identify areas to restore to SAP Best Practice processes.

Once all plans of data migration of the sandbox system are complete the environment is planned for validation.

Some of the deliverables or activities to note are as follows: custom code assessment and cleanup activities; data volume strategy and planning; design and configuration for quick wins.

The methodology detail will inform how to set up **Data Volume Management (DVM)** in the system environment and how to use **Early Watch Alert (EWA)** reports to indicate the need for this DVM.

Areas to EXPLORE for System Conversion

a. **Application:** Identify and design functional quick wins (e.g. implementation of Operational Reporting), and SAP S/4 HANA functionality in scope of the conversion project.

b. **Custom Code and Data volume management:** We want to minimize the amount of custom code that is brought over to the SAP S/4HANA system that will then need to be maintained with the solution.

We want to execute a conversion of the Sandbox environment (migration on to SAP HANA and the system conversion to SAP S/4HANA). The tasks are detailed in project accelerators, such as the SAP S/4HANA admin guide.

c. **System & Data Migration:** The conversion of the SAP systems (Sandbox, supporting systems, and production) to SAP S/4 HANA are planned. The conversion includes the activation of solution, and the conversion of the business data into the new and simplified business data format.

   We will execute a conversion of the sandbox environment in this phase.

d. **Technical Architecture & Infrastructure:** SAP S/4 HANA comes with SAP HANA as the underlying data base. The introduction of SAP HANA in your data center needs to be properly planned based on business and IT requirements.

Key Deliverables

a. Training strategy
b. Sandbox
c. Design for the Gaps and Deltas
d. Custom code analysis
e. Test plan
f. Legacy data migration design and plan
g. Setup of sandbox and DEV environment
h. Initial sizing
i. Technical design
j. Operations impact evaluation.
k. Testing strategy

4.3 Realize Phase

The Realize phase is the logical continuation of the work that was done in the Explore phase.

- IT Infrastructure will be set up.
- Systems and applications will be configured, tested, and validated.
- Training will be prepared and enabled.
- Custom code will be adjusted and data aging configured.
- Nonproductive systems will be migrated to the new environment.
- Tools and operations support processes will be set up.

The configuration activities for any adjustments based on the initial analysis in the sandbox need to be done. The initial analysis is based on the different business priorities, such as core finance, audit cash, customer service, buying the product, and other business priorities.

Accelerators provide additional guidance & links for developers on how to adjust custom code and how to structure adjustment activities.

In this phase you are doing a nonproductive system conversion of the DEV and QAS systems. This includes the testing cutover procedure and simulation. So, incrementally as you convert each system, each landscape, you are validating that every adjustment that is made, can be carried forward and improve the cutover timelines. You need to minimize the cutover time and make sure that all the adjustments are done and finalized before you go into the deploy phase.

Key Deliverables

a. Training enabled
b. Configurations and Product enhancements
c. Data aging configurations
d. Custom code management execution
e. Test execution
f. Cutover preparation
g. Sizing and scalability verification
h. IT infrastructure set up & Test
i. Operations implementation
j. Integration validation
k. Custom code management
l. Data aging configuration
m. Data migration and verification
n. Data aging configuration

4.4 Deploy Phase

Purpose - To finalize readiness of SAP S/4 HANA and its supporting tools and processes for production go live.

It includes the following activities:

- Final testing,

- End User training
- Cutover rehearsal
- IT infrastructure and operations finalization
- Conversion of the productive SAP ERP to SAP S/4 HANA.
- Handover all activities to the customer and close the project.

Similar to other journeys to SAP S/4HANA, there are relatively few deliverables in this phase.

Before running the production conversion, the users are trained, cutover *dress rehearsals / mock cutovers* are completed. The operations team are ready to provide functional and technical support and all final checks cleared and ready for production conversion, load, and run. With support transitioning to the operations team.

As we transition into operations, we have activities which look after the '*Hyper Care*' / '*post go-live*' Support, Incident analysis and Handover to Support Organization and Management in the support organization.

Key Deliverables

a. End user training

b. Dress rehearsal

c. IT infrastructure finalization

d. Operation readiness

e. Cutover to production

4.5 Additional Information

Key deliverables for RUN phase are

a. Handover to support organization

b. Hyper care support

c. Project closing

The last action in the DEPLOY phase is to finalise the Project Closeout Report and obtain closeout sign-off from the key stakeholder representing the application and operations.

For Project Closing, Key Deliverables are:

- Closing

NOTES

NOTES

NOTES

NOTES

NOTES

NOTES

CHAPTER 5

Journey Landscape Transformation for SAP S/4 HANA

The SAP S/4HANA family and transition paths

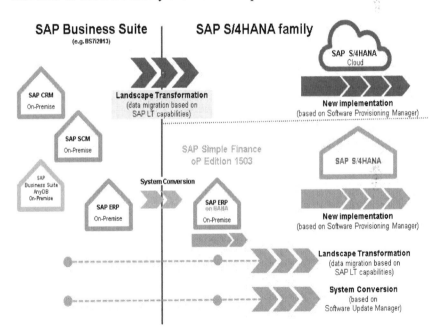

Figure 5.1 JOURNEY Landscape Transformation for SAP S/4HANA >
The SAP S/4HANA Family and Transition Paths

Image Source: SAP SE / AG

In SAP S/4HANA, we can follow different paths.

There are countless options for landscape transformation. It is not a single scenario but a combination of different scenarios that can be implemented.

Whenever we discuss landscape transformation, we also discuss system conversion and new implementation. This is the reason that the system conversion roadmap in the roadmap viewer contains landscape transformation elements.

Now, let's discuss *Transition to SAP S/4HANA, Landscape Transformation*.

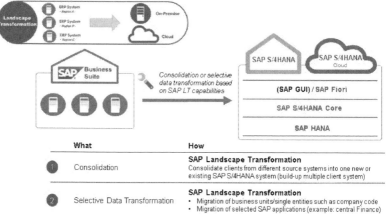

Figure 5.2 Transition to SAP S/4HANA, Landscape Transformation

Image Source: SAP SE / AG

The figure shows the scenario where customers want to consolidate their landscape or to selectively transform data into a SAP S/4HANA system.

Some of the benefits from this scenario might be:

a. **Value-based migration**: selective data transformation allows a phased approach focusing the first SAP S/4HANA migration phase on parts of the business with highest ROI and lowest TCI.

b. **Agility**: stay on current business processes but move gradually to SAP S/4HANA innovations (Move to SAP S/4HANA at your own pace!)

c. **TCO reduction**: system and landscape consolidation with harmonized/simplified processes and unified master data lead to lower cost of operations.

Major Elements in Transition Process

Three major elements are involved in the transition process from the *starting system release* to SAP S/4HANA as follows:

a. Preparation (in the starting/current systems)

b. Technical implementation

c. Semantical adoption.

SAP S/4HANA Data Migration / Landscape Transformation Platform

SAP S/4HANA Data Migration / Landscape Transformation Platform

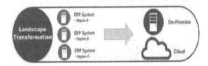

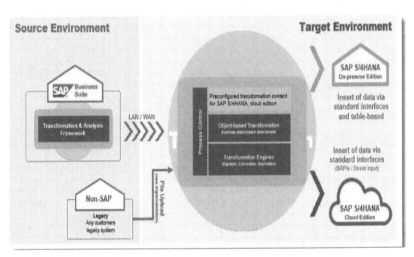

Figure 5.3 SAP S/4HANA Data Migration / Landscape Transformation Platform

Image Source: SAP SE / AG

Three pre-configured data migration requirements may be needed in a specific landscape transformation:

a. Consolidation
b. Migration of business units
c. Migration of selected applications

5.1 Landscape Transformation in the PREPARE Phase

Key Deliverables

a. Transition planning
b. Transition preparation

Tasks

a. Transition planning
   - Define the Data Migration architecture
b. Transition preparation
   - Execute on follow-ups from transition planning

5.2 Landscape Transformation in the EXPLORE Phase

Key Deliverables

a. Project delivery platform setup
b. Data migration design

Tasks

a. Project delivery platform setup
   - Setup landscape transformation software (only LT scenarios)
b. Data migration design
   - Run a Landscape transformation assessment (only LT scenarios).

There are two landscape transformation specific tasks in the EXPLORE phase.

The task to *Run a Landscape Transformation Assessment* is described as follows:

Changing business requirements continuously drive organizations to realign and restructure their business. As a consequence, the transformation of SAP landscapes has become an on-going business for SAP customers with a strategic importance to stay agile and competitive. Instead of replacing legacy environments by using generic or self-made tools and technologies, SAP customers can use SAP Landscape Transformation as a cost-efficient and secure alternative. SAP customers can manage their SAP-related transformation requirements in a holistic manner - reflecting organizational changes, acquisitions of companies, divestitures, or the harmonization of processes and data in their existing SAP system landscape.

The objective of this task is to run a Landscape Transformation Assessment together with SAP. The scenarios in scope are as follows:

    a. Client transfer

    b. System merge

    c. Company code transfer

5.3 Landscape Transformation in the REALIZE Phase

Key Deliverables

    a. Data migration and verification

    b. Cutover preparation.

Tasks

    a. Perform Client Transfer (LT scenario – Client transfer)

    b. Perform Company code transfer (LT scenario – Company code transfer)

    c. Create Cutover Plan (Landscape transformation – Client transfer)

5.4 Landscape Transformation in the DEPLOY Phase

Key Deliverables

    a. Dress rehearsal

    b. Production cutover

Tasks

Production Cutover (Landscape transformation)

NOTES

NOTES

NOTES

NOTES

NOTES

NOTES

CHAPTER 6

SAP S/4 HANA and SAP Activate – Top 410 Plus Interview Questions and Answers

1. How SAP Activate keep team members aligned and informed?

Ans: By means of daily team stand-up meeting.

2. For delivering Agile projects what activities are most critical?

Ans: a) Sprint planning

b) Release planning

3. In any Agile project in the backlog who prioritize the user stories?

Ans: Product Owner

4. Explain, in a nutshell, the benefits of the SAP best practices?

Ans: a) Fast time to value

b) Predictable results

c) Simple on-boarding to cloud

5. Which content is made available once you activated SAP Best Practices for a new financial implementation?

Ans: a) Pre-configured business processes

b) Standard chart of accounts

6. What is the count of minimum number of quality gates recommended in Activate?

Ans: 4

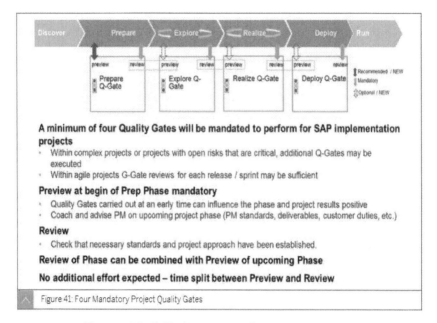

Figure 41: Four Mandatory Project Quality Gates

Figure 6.1 SAP Activate quality gates overview

Image source – SAP AG / SE

7. The Transformation Strategy completion is being done in which phase of SAP Activate methodology?

Ans: Prepare

8. During post cutover what SAP Activate usually use to do?

Ans: Submit email-address via online form

9. Cut-over Rehearsal completion is being done in which phase of SAP Activate methodology?

Ans: Deploy

10. For New Implementation Cloud, name the last process flow step of the realization phase?

Ans: Transition to Operations to Production Support Plan

11. To estimate the relative size of the backlog, what technique a project team can use?

Ans: Planning Poker

12. In the Roadmap Viewer, name the most granular view?

Ans: Deliverables and/or Accelerators

13. In SAP Activate the Blueprint phase is replaced by which phase?

Ans: **VALIDATE SOLUTION**

Validate to best practices with fit/gap workshops, capture delta.

14. In SAP Activate name the three Pillars names?

Ans: a. SAP Best-Practices

b. Guided Configuration

c. Methodology.

15. Explain the common road blockers while Applying Agile to ERP projects?

Ans:

a. A new way to manage projects

- Makes all the dysfunction in a team or organization visible
- Bad products will be delivered sooner with poor First Time Right Product quality, and will cause faster failure for doomed projects
- People may follow the mechanics without following the values of Agile

b. People are most comfortable with what they know

- ERP project team members have an attachment to Waterfall development
- Lack of talent recognition mechanisms (like, award, incentives) for increasing delivery speed

c. ERP configuration is NOT programming

d. Management of development objects integrated with sprint delivery

e. Integrating off-shore development

f. Lack / poor sequencing of user stories, tasks, activities, and poor management of dependencies

g. Encompassing & integrated ERP solutions

- Integrated end-to-end business processes are difficult to decompose

16. How you can address the common road blockers while applying Agile to ERP projects?

Ans:

- Assessing agile readiness
- Tailor the approach to the adoption lifecycle
- Identify the case for change
- Identify a champion for Agile
- Change in roles and responsibilities
- Select the right first project -demonstrate success
- Set realistic expectations of delivery
- Build a GREAT backlog
- Integrate organizational change management

17. Tell some key lessons learned while applying Agile to ERP projects?

Ans:

a. Be proactive in creating a model which works for the organizational culture
b. Varying steps of adoption needs to be considered
c. Find the Agile Champion
d. Be proactive in selecting the right first project, not all projects are good candidates for Agile
e. Train the team at all levels
f. Develop a willing to work Product Council
g. Find the right Product Owner
h. Give more focus on team work rather than mechanics
i. Collaboration over co-location
j. Build effectively the Backlog – Story Mapping and Stories
k. Set rules to make productive optimum team engagement
l. Selecting the proper metrics and the proper reporting tools
m. Process validated Lean Agile processes are incremental, iterative, and adaptive

- Team was not disrupted by the scope changes

- Team generally made change adoption in just 3-4 sprints

n. Key Project / Program stakeholders

- Confirm empirical evidence is better than Progress Reports
- Give proper slack time to teams and allow proper time in Scrum planning events to focus on *Value Add* work
- Team becomes *Being Agile* mindset and *Lean Thinkers* rather than just *doing Agile*
- Work products completed significantly ahead of stipulated project milestone time

18. Explain critical success factors for an Agile SAP team?

Ans:

- Establish *Buy-In* to the process at all levels
- Establish confidence and proactively start with win-win situation and do something that can deliver a quick win –
- The *Art of Storytelling*
- Do not be discouraged at the moment of *First Awkward Use*
- Integrating members of team that are not co-located
- Ability to remove impediments
- Manage the flow of work
- Establish a process and framework that works best with your culture, resources, and environment
- Continuously update process and framework –Learn and Adjust

19. What are the key characteristics (6) of Activate?

Ans:

a. **START WITH BEST PRACTICES**

   Use ready-to run business processes

b. **VALIDATE SOLUTION**

   Validate to best practices with fit/gap workshops, capture delta

c. **MODULAR, SCALABLE AND AGILE**

   Structure project to deliver the solution incrementally

d. **CLOUD READY**

Leverage the flexibility and speed of the cloud

e. **PREMIUM ENGAGEMENT READY**

Build and Run fully supported

via SAP control centers

f. **QUALITY BUILT-IN**

Identify risk early with total quality approach

20. What view is available under phase in Roadmap Viewer?

Ans: a. Phase
    b. Work-stream
    c. Deliverable

21. What tools are there to support guided configuration source?

Ans: a. Solution Builder
    b. Self-Service UIs
    c. Expert Configuration

22. What are the deliverables for customer team enablement?

Ans: a. Self-enablement
    b. Customer team learning plan
    c. Knowledge transfer

23. When does the project team formally hear the communication that the Product Owner approved the prioritized backlog?

Ans: Upon completion of the deliverable, *Design for Gaps and Deltas* in the EXPLORE Phase of Solution Design. This comes before release and sprint planning.

24. What are the activities / deliverables in the Preparation Phase for New Cloud Implementation?

Ans: a. Customer Team Self Enablement
    b. Project Initiation and Governance
    c. Project Plans, Schedule, and budget
    d. Project standards and infrastructure
    e. Project Kick-off and On-Boarding
    f. Phase Closure

25. What phase is the handover to support task?

Ans: Deploy Phase

26. What is the purpose of SCRUM of SCRUMs?

Ans: Scrum of Scrums focuses on integration topics and cohesive solution build. It consists of the lead consultants and product owners from the individual scrum teams.

27. What are the phases of the methodology?

We've worked to bring in the simplicity of cloud implementation while retaining content required for on premise projects. We've struck a balance using these four phases:

- **Prepare:** The project is initiated and planned, including quality, and risk plans. The system environment is set up, including best practices for ready-to-run processes.
- **Explore:** The customer team explores SAP solution capabilities while the system integrator researches the customer's business. Together, they use fit/gap workshops to identify the configuration and extensions that best meet customer requirements.
- **Realize:** The team configures and extends the system, based on prioritizing the requirements captured in the Explore phase. Configuration and build are done in short cycles, ensuring regular validation and feedback from the business. Structured testing and data migration activities ensure quality.
- **Deploy:** Final preparations before cutover to production ensure that that the system, users, and data are ready for transition to productive use. The transition to operations includes setting up and launching support, then handing off operations to the organization managing the environment.

Note:

- **Discover:** what resources are available before a SAP S/4HANA project starts.
- **Prepare:** infrastructure is set up and selected SAP Best Practices are activated.
- **Explore:** workshops define the solution and use SAP Best Practice processes.

- **Realize:** implementation is undertaken tracking all work in SAP Solution Manager.
- **Deploy:** SAP Solution Manager is used in the production cutover.
- **Run:** SAP Solution Manager is used to monitor and optimize the solution.

28. What are the flow diagram of SAP Activate methodology new implementation and system conversion?

Ans:

SAP Activate

New Implementation

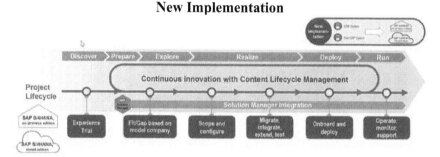

Figure 6.2 SAP Activate new implementation flow diagram
Image source – SAP AG / SE

System Conversion

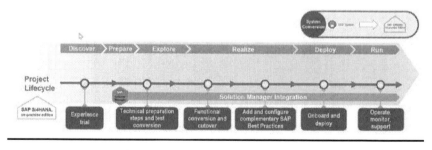

Figure 6.3 SAP Activate new implementation flow diagram
Image source – SAP AG / SE

29. Explain SAP Activate Methodology Principles?

   a. Start with best practices: Make the effective use of ready to run business processes

    b. Cloud ready: Utilize the speed and flexibility of the cloud

    c. Validate solution: With fit-gap workshops, capture delta and validate best practices

    d. Premium engagement ready: Via SAP control centers build and run fully supported features

    e. Modular, scalable and agile: Plan / prioritize project to deliver the end to end solution incrementally

    f. Quality built-in: Identify risk early with total quality approach

30. How Agile and Lean act as a good combination?

Ans: Where Agile focuses on the delivery of the software and systems, lean focuses on the optimization of the entire business operation. In organizations that use lean methods, all operating processes are tuned to each other to the maximum. Unnecessary procedures, bottlenecks, and other obstacles are removed where possible to facilitate an optimum *flow*. It plays an important function for lean success. Just like lean, Agile is based on the premise that the people on the work floor are the best people to say how their work can be carried out better. The flexibility of Agile forms an excellent basis for a lean operating organization, just as speed, flexibility and focus on customer value.

30. What are the main benefits of Agile implementation in SAP Project?

Ans: **a. Faster results**

- Iterative and incremental way of delivery of shippable products features based on customer priority in 1-4 weeks duration sprints
- CAST score from Product owner / customer feedback after each sprint

b. Increased flexibility

- Can respond to changes per *sprint*
- Use of relevant extreme programming and DevOps best practices, like, Continuous build, deployment, integration, test driven development, pair programming, refactoring during software products delivery
- Continuous communication, collaboration, and integration with business from day one ,

c. More transparency

- Monthly metrics data trend analysis
- Sprint Reviews for checking the results and requirements
- Risks are quickly identified and therefore manageable

- Daily stand-up meetings for the DEV team
- Continuous communication, collaboration, and integration with business from day one.

31. Explain one DEMO diagram of Agile implementation in SAP Project?

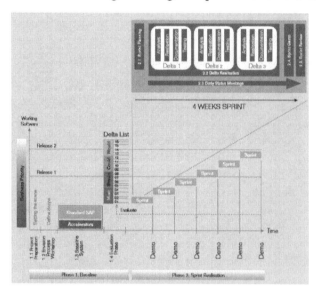

Figure 6.4 DEMO diagram of Agile implementation in SAP Project
Image source – SAP AG / SE

32. What are SAP Activate building blocks?

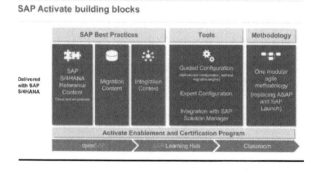

Figure 6.5 SAP Activate building blocks overview
Image source – SAP AG / SE

33. When does the DEV team receive formal feedback from the product owner?

Ans: During the sprint review

34. To access the SAP Activate Methodology content in the Roadmap Viewer which navigation option do you use?

Ans: Navigate by work stream

35. When does the team complete the System Assessment in AP Activate Methodology?

Ans: Prepare

36. Name the component of SAP Activate which offers customers a reference solution in the cloud for a quick start?

Ans: SAP Best Practices

37. In the Explore Phase during the Scope Validation/Fit-Gap Analysis activity which accelerations can you use?

Ans: a. RICEF specification template

      b. Solution validation workshop

38. For SAP Activate on-premise in the SAP Jam space what is the hierarchy level under Phase?

Ans: Key Deliverable

39. In the Prepare Phase what are the tasks required?

Ans: a. Train the project team

      b. Set up the infrastructure to support the project

      c. Identify relevant SAP Best Practices

40. What is the main purpose of a sprint retrospective meeting?

Ans: Improve the SCRUM process

41. When does the team identify and design functional quick wins in scope of the conversion project in SAP Activate methodology?

Ans: Explore

42. In SAP Activate Methodology name the key characteristics of the implementation approach?

Ans: a. Premium engagement ready

      b. Validate solution

      c. Start with SAP Best Practices

43. Name the accelerator which can help you to document the detailed design of solution extensions?

Ans: RICEF Specification Template

44. What is SAP S/4 HANA?

SAP HANA (High-Performance Analytical Appliance) is an in-memory database engine from SAP that is used to analyze large data sets in real time that reside entirely in memory. Very crudely it is a database system which totally changes the DBMS methodology and it can be deployable on premises or over cloud.

45. What are SAP S/4HANA goals?

HANA Goals

- Enables new application and optimize existing application
- High performance and scalability
- Hybrid data management system
- Compatible with standard DBMS feature
- Support for text analysis, indexing, and search
- Cloud support and application isolation
- Executing application logic inside the data layer

46. What are the currently available SAP S/4HANA deployment options?

Ans: SAP currently plans to offer on-premise, cloud (public and managed), and hybrid deployments.

47. Name the technologies from which SAP HANA evolved?

Ans: By combining earlier developed technologies, BW Accelerator and Max DB with its in-memory capabilities SAP HANA evolved.

48. What is the benefit to the data model for using an in-memory platform?

Ans: SAP S/4HANA delivers **high-volume transaction processing**

(OLTP) and **high volume real-time analytical processes (OLAP)** based on a unified data model without the redundant data layers typically required by traditional RDBMS based systems. This reduces TCO while providing new opportunities to increase business value from existing investments. Examples for redundant data layers are custom-built layers based on database tuning efforts such as secondary indexes, or application built-in performance accelerators such as aggregate tables or multiple general ledger versions for different managerial reporting needs.

The massive simplifications of the data model and the data processing layers enable business and technological innovations on a broad scale across all lines-of-business and industry solutions. The new application architecture simplifies system landscape architectures and accelerates cloud deployments on an economical scale.

49. In simple finance, can I have a new field based on business need which can link with logistics? For example, a team field which will drive from sales Oder which will flow to GL posting?

Ans: You can add a field to the universal journal easily but you will have to create derivation logic of some kind to fill it and as with any derivation the more complex you make the logic to fill it, the more you'll impact performance during posting.

50. Can customers run different sap s/4hana editions in parallel in their enterprise architecture?

Ans: Yes. sap s/4 hana editions are integrated and run mostly on the same data semantic.

51. What are the key benefits of sap s/4hana?

Ans: SAP s/4hana delivers **high volume transaction processing (OLTP)** and **high volume real time analytical processes (OLAP)** based on unified data model without the redundant data layers.

52. Explain the Fit/Gap Workshops diagram in Explore phase of SAP Activate methodology?

Ans:

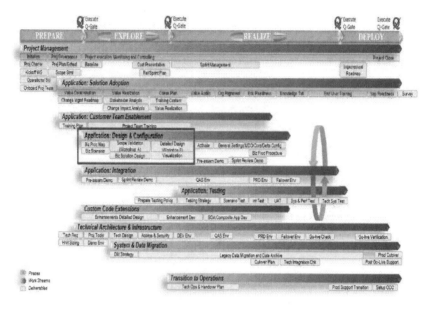

Figure 6.6 Fit/Gap Workshops diagram in Explore phase of SAP Activate methodology

Image Source: SAP SE / AG

53. What is the purpose of Fit/Gap Analysis?

Ans:

- The primary objective is to have an updated and approved Scope Baseline to move into the Realization phase
- Validate pre-activated or pre-assembled solution in sandbox system
- Drive towards adopting SAP standard processes
- Ensure that SAP implementation meets customer's business needs
- Discover, clarify, and negotiate solution design
- Identify and capture delta business requirements and gaps (on top of the initial Sandbox system)
- Prioritize delta requirements and gaps
- Prevent the need for rework during realization.

54. Outline the key steps of Fit/Gap Analysis in Explore phase?

Ans: Prepare for Fit/Gap Analysis

- Download and review Best Practices documentation relevant for the project (based on SOW and Scope Statement)
- Setup Sandbox System based on CAL appliance (http://cal.sap.com) (or Activate Best Practices if not using CAL)
- Consultants to review Best Practices functionality in Sandbox and configure system for workshops (quick wins, customer specific org. units and master data)

B. Conduct WS A–Validate Solution

- Set expectations with the business users; tie all discussion to business value and benefits
- Demonstrate the standard processes and guide customer towards adopting standard
- Identify and document delta requirements and gaps
- Prioritize all delta requirements and gaps

C. Conduct WS B–Conduct Delta Design Workshops

- Prepare solution design for the identified delta requirements and gaps
- Visualize application for areas that require changes

D. Prepare Release and Sprint plan for Realize phase

- Prioritize Backlog with delta requirements and gaps
- Estimate relative effort of all changes
- Prepare Release and Sprint plan for Realize phase

55. Explain one key example of validate solution?

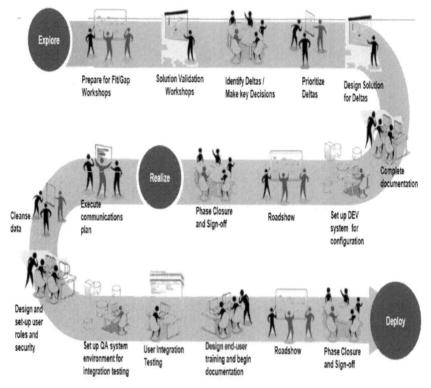

Figure 6.7 Validate solution key example

Image Source: SAP SE / AG

56. Explain Checklist: Prepare for Fit/Gap Analysis Workshops?

Ans:

a. All the project team members need to understand the project scope (review SOW and Scope Statement)

b. Download and review Best Practices documentation relevant for the project (based on SOW and Scope Statement)

c. Setup sandbox system based on CAL appliance (or Activate Best Practices if not using CAL). Activation guidance using both methods can be found in the *Activate Best Practices* pages in the Reference Guide

d. In sandbox consultants needs to cross check Best Practices outcome and configure system for workshops (quick wins, customer specific org. units and master data). Additional details can be found in the *Test SAP Best Practice Activation* page in the Reference Guide.

e. Schedule workshops (book rooms, invite participants, explain purpose/goals)

f. Prepare workshop artifacts (templates to showcase results, slides to run workshop, confirm system is configured, and confirm access to process flows)

57. Give some examples of project accelerators in SAP Activate methodology?

Ans:

- **Customer presentation**: overview presentation of Edition
- **Content Library**: web page with links to all the content in the Edition
- **Project schedule**: example implementation project schedule
- **Prerequisite matrix**: relationship between Scope Items and Building Blocks
- **Delivery supplement**: key implementation information
- **Admin Guide for SAP S/4HANA & SAP Note***: detailed instructions
- **Software and delivery requirements***: precise software releases required
- **Master Data Overview**: describes master data used in the Edition
- SCII, SLIN, SE30, ST05
- HP ALM test plan and test lab, Focus tool for automating test scripts

58. Mention the key functions of SAP Solution manager in SAP Activate methodology?

Ans: Customers can choose which capabilities of SAP Solution Manger to use in their project. For any on-premise or hybrid implementation the following capabilities can be used:

- **Business requirements and IT requirements**: Central storage of requirements
- **Project management**: For your implementation plan and manage the schedule and consultants.

- **Process management**: With a new user interface and integrated process diagram editor, SAP Solution Manager 7.2 provides a new way to manage end user business processes
- **Change and release management**: Provide change deployment control and risk mitigation
- **Test management**: Keeping track of all test scripts, test cases and test results, test and deploy your SAP S/4HANA solution

59. Explain the general validation workshop principles?

Ans: Workshop best practice should still be followed:

- Preparation of meetings with customer business leads to allow them for their business and processes introduction. Allow consultants to prepare workshops (not a detailed as-is analysis).
- Prepare agenda for the workshop and chalk out the action items. Proactively mitigate the risks &/or issues within stipulated timeframe.
- Set boundaries at start of each workshop.
- At start of each workshop provide process, value, and strategic context.
- Continuously focus on business value added process improvement activities using PDCA cycle.
- Ensure process diagrams include roles (swim lanes): this helps business to engage.
- Prioritize scope and gaps.
- For new processes document decisions, assumptions, and business risks & impacts.
- Produce detailed documentation immediately.
- Formal sign-off of the Gap List before realize phase starts.

60. Why does SAP need a new methodology *SAP Activate*?

Ans: The traditional Waterfall model has many pitfalls in current market with varying complex customer requirements. SAP Activate Methodology is a harmonized Agile implementation approach for cloud, on premise, and hybrid deployments for delivering shippable product increments in an iterative and incremental way.

Purpose and Goal of SAP Activate

- Shorten time to value

- Reduce risks
- Flexibility and choice
- Start with best practices
- Cloud ready
- Validate solution
- Modular, Scalable, and Agile
- Quality built in

61. What components or tools does SAP Activate methodology include?

Ans: The SAP Activate methodology contains accelerators, tools, templates, questionnaires, checklists, work streams, and guidebooks to ensure efficient, consistent, and repeatable delivery of SAP implementations and upgrades.

62. What environments is SAP Activate methodology best suited for?

Ans: SAP Activate Methodology is a harmonized Agile implementation approach for on-premise, cloud, and hybrid deployments for delivering shippable product increments in an iterative and incremental way. It contains guided configuration and transition scenario guidance, covering scenarios such as new Implementation, system conversion, and landscape transformation. The methodology scales extremely well, becoming more robust for larger programs / projects or lightweight for smaller engagements.

63. Who can use the SAP Activate methodology?

Ans: Anybody in any organization, customer, business having proper license to use SAP Activate methodology. You may use SAP Activate methodology on your own, or while you are working with SAP or as a SAP partner. It's completely your choice.

With Cloud based access you can view the contents or may engage with others in the community and can give valuable feedback to the teams building & tuning the methodology content.

64. After the introduction of new SAP Activate methodology what may happen to the ASAP and SAP Launch Methodologies?

Ans: In past SAP offered ASAP for managed cloud implementations and on-premise implementations, also SAP offered SAP Launch for public cloud implementations.

The two began to converge after the introduction of ASAP's *assemble to order* approach. But still cloud and on premise implementations differ in capabilities, technology, scope, and solution flexibility. Now SAP Activate aligns on-premise implementations and cloud implementation for clients ready to adopt SAP S/4HANA.

65. What are user options for using the SAP activate methodology?

Parameter	Old	Replaced with / New	Main improvements
New Implementation	ASAP 8.0	SAP Activate methodology for On Premise edition	– Agile Project delivery, iterative & incremental – Use of SAP best practices – Reduced Project life cycle
New Implementation	SAP Launch	SAP Activate methodology for cloud edition	– SAP BluePrint activities replaced with solution fit/gap workshops – Guided configuration
System Conversion & Landscape transformation	-	SAP Activate methodology for System Conversion / Landscape transformation (planned)	– Upto 10 key deliverables per phase and easier access to accelerators and key guides

66. What do you mean by SAP Activate?

Ans: SAP Activate is the first Agile and S4/HANA focused methodology for SAP projects. It is one simple, modular and Agile methodology supporting all S/4 HANA transition scenarios.

In short, SAP Activate is a combination of SAP Best Practices, SAP guided configuration, and Agile methodology which allows building smart and simplify the adoption of SAP S/4 HANA. SAP Activate gives the freedom to run fast with Fiori UX and with a lower TCO and continuous innovation with built-in extensibility to fit different needs. The key take away will be that SAP Activate is one methodology for any deployment mode - cloud, hybrid, on premise, or mobile for S\4 HANA.

It provides best practices for migration, integration, and configuration for SAP S/4 HANA. It supports different starting points for customers to adopt SAP S/4 HANA – new implementation, system conversion and landscape transformation.

67. What are the main 2 variants of SAP Activate Implementation Methodology?

Ans: a. **On-Premise**: Used for new implementation of S/4 HANA On-Premise editions and other SAP applications.

  b. **Cloud**: Used for implementation of S/4 HANA Cloud edition, SAP SuccessFactors, and other SAP applications. Here the new system installation & management occur outside of the project.

68. What are the main three focus elements of SAP Activate Methodology?

  a. SAP best practices

  b. Guided configuration

  c. One methodology

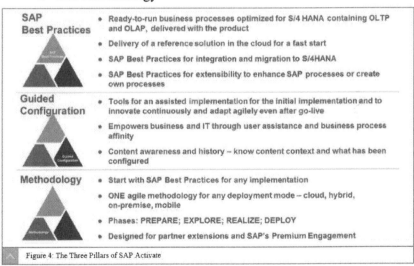

SAP Best Practices	• Ready-to-run business processes optimized for S/4 HANA containing OLTP and OLAP, delivered with the product
	• Delivery of a reference solution in the cloud for a fast start
	• SAP Best Practices for integration and migration to S/4HANA
	• SAP Best Practices for extensibility to enhance SAP processes or create own processes
Guided Configuration	• Tools for an assisted implementation for the initial implementation and to innovate continuously and adapt agilely even after go-live
	• Empowers business and IT through user assistance and business process affinity
	• Content awareness and history – know content context and what has been configured
Methodology	• Start with SAP Best Practices for any implementation
	• ONE agile methodology for any deployment mode – cloud, hybrid, on-premise, mobile
	• Phases: PREPARE; EXPLORE; REALIZE; DEPLOY
	• Designed for partner extensions and SAP's Premium Engagement

Figure 4: The Three Pillars of SAP Activate

Figure 6.8 Three Pilar of SAP Activate methodology

Image source: SAP AG / SE

69. Explain SAP Best Practices of SAP Activate Methodology in a nutshell?

Ans:

- SAP delivers ready-to-run business processes that are optimized for SAP S/4 HANA containing OLTP and OLAP, delivered with the product.
- It has best practices for integration, migration, and extensibility to expand the existing processes with the customer's own processes.
- It has delivery of a reference solution in the cloud for a fast start.
- Continuous process of improvement of SAP SuccessFactors Best Practices.
- It has the below aspects.

a) Fast time to value

  - Deploy SAP innovations fast, simple, and flexible
  - Get a jump-start for your implementations with SAP best practices

b) Predictable results

  - Leverage preconfigured business content
  - Use SAP's tested and proven methodology with prescriptive guidelines

c) Simple On-boarding to cloudProtect on-premise investments with extensions to the cloud

  - Move up on the path to the cloud from pre-assembled pilots to productive use

SAP Best Practices help project teams accelerate time to value. They provide content that helps jump-start the implementation with read-to-run processes and other assets.

The Best Practices contain rich business scenarios and business content. This helps customers get predictable and repeatable results from the Best Practices. The Best Practices and some additional set up, (for example, personalization, additional configuration or enhancements of the pre-delivered content), can be used as a baseline for an implementation project.

Best Practices can be deployed in the cloud which further improves flexibility and time to value.

70. Explain Guided Configuration of SAP Activate Methodology in a nutshell?

Ans: SAP Activate Guided configuration is a new approach for an assisted way to implement SAP Best Practices. For SAP S/4HANA Cloud edition, it also facilitates the lifecycle management of the pre-configured business processes from SAP and any additional customizing added by the customer. SAP is providing various tools to support these efforts.

Tools to assist rapid implementation such as SAP SuccessFactors Administration Tool and Setup Wizards.

- The guided configuration system is now available in the cloud.

- For customers or expert users who can command and configure a solution, there are tools for an assisted implementation that provide a self-service configuration user experience.

- These tools empower business users to configure the environment and make it much easier to configure. The configuration tables are in IMG.

- The guided configuration also offers capabilities for what we call content lifecycle management. This essentially involves looking at the configuration settings and ensuring that the configuration settings that are set in that solution are not impacted by a new version of best practices or a new version of processes that are being shipped in the next release of the SAP solution. This is extremely important in the cloud where the release cycle is much more compressed.

- SAP S/4HANA comes with new capabilities and new functionality every quarter. The pace of change and innovation that the customers are getting through the cloud solutions is much higher than what we would see with on-premise solutions. So with cloud solutions it is important to use the guided configuration tools.

71. Why we need SAP Activate?

Ans:

Benefits

- Enable consistent project delivery, reduce complexity, and increases quality by providing common framework and language for all SAP project.

- Broad product coverage, including support for SAP SuccessFactors and all transition scenarios to SAP S/4HANA.

- Scalable, supports all sizes of projects, from small fast cloud deployments to comprehensive global deployments in on-premise and hybrid environment.
- Prescriptive and comprehensive – provides guided work procedures for project team members, deliverables for project managers and accelerators like how-to documents and templates for all users.
- Accelerates project delivery through use of SAP Best Practices, fit/gap analysis, Agile project management, application visualization, and use of Cloud technology.

  •Methodology foundation fully aligned with proven project management practice of Project Management Institute, like formal Quality, Risk, and Issues Management.

72. What are software inspections (reviews)?

Ans:

- Meetings (real or virtual) during which designs and code are reviewed by people other than the original developer.

73. What are the benefits of inspections?

Ans:

a. New perspective

- Finding defects may be easier for people who haven't seen the artifact before and don't have preconceived ideas about its correctness.

b. Knowledge sharing

- Regarding designs and specific software artifacts
- Regarding defect detection practices

c. Find flaws early

- Can dramatically reduce cost of fixing them
- During detail design –even before code is written
- Or code that does not yet have a test harness
- Or code in which testing has found flaws but root causes are not understood
- Reduce rework and testing effort
- Can reduce overall development effort

74. What attributes are well-handled by inspections but not testing?

Ans:

a. Characteristics of code
   - Maintainability, evaluability, reusability
b. Other properties tough to test
   - Scalability, efficiency
   - Security, integrity
   - Robustness, reliability, exception handling
c. Requirements, architecture, design documents
   - Cannot *execute* these as a test

75. Explain different kinds of inspections?

Ans:

a. Inspections / Formal Technical Reviews

I. Participation defined by policy
   - Developers
   - Designated key individuals –peers, QA team, Review Board, etc.

II. Advance preparation by participants
   - Typically based on checklists

III. Formal meeting to discuss artifact
   - Led by moderator, not author
   - Documented process followed
   - May be virtual or conferenced

IV. Formal follow-up process
   - Written deliverable from review
   - Appraise product

b. Walkthroughs
   - No advance preparation
   - Author leads discussion in meeting
   - No formal follow-up

- Low cost, valuable for education

c. Other review approaches

- Pass-around –preparation part of an inspection
- Peer desk check –examination by a single reviewer (like pair programming)
- Ad-hoc –informal feedback from a team member

d. There are tradeoffs among the techniques

- Formal reviews typically find more bugs
- Ford Motor: 50% more bugs found
- But they also cost more

76. Who are the key stakeholders in inspection?

Ans: Moderator and recorder

77. Explain moderator key responsibility?

Ans: Moderator organizes review

- Keeps discussion on track
- Ensures follow-up happens

78. Explain Moderator key characteristics?

Ans:

Key characteristics

- Good facilitator
- Knowledgeable
- Impartial and respected
- Can hold participants accountable and correct the inappropriate behavior

79. Explain Recorder key responsibility?

Ans: Recorder captures a log of the inspection process.

80. Explain reader key responsibility?

Ans: Reader presents material

- Describes interpretation of each point
- Discuss different interpretations by other team members

81. Why should the Reader be different from the Author?

Ans: Reader reveals ambiguities

- If author were to present, others might not mention that their interpretation was different

82. Explain Author key responsibility?

Ans: Author describes rationale for work.

- Not moderator or reader
- Conflict between objectivity required of moderator/reader and advocacy for the author's own work
- Others raise issues more comfortably

83. In SAP HANA what are the main components?

Ans:

SAP HANA main components are as follows:

a. SAP **In-Memory database (IMDB)**

b. In-memory computing Studio and

c. Data replication components (SLT, BODS, and so on.).

84. In SAP HANA tell the basic technology concepts?

Ans:

a. In-memory where data resides on main memory rather than on disk,

b. Column based database, data compression and pushing application logic to DATABASE layer,

c. Parallel processing and Multi-Core CPUs to leverage new Hardware technology.

85. Explain the main benefit of In-memory in SAP HANA?

Ans:

Accessing data from main memory is much faster than accessing data on a disk.

86. In SAP HANA what degree of data compression is expected?

Ans: The degree of data compression depends on the number of unique values in the data. The fewer the unique values, the better is the data compression.

87. What are the top use cases in SAP HANA?

The top use cases in SAP HANA are as follows:

  a. Real-time financial planning

  b. Customer segmentation

  c. Genome analysis

  d. Profitability analysis and

  e. Detective HANA

88. Explain an example of SAP HANA architecture?

Ans:

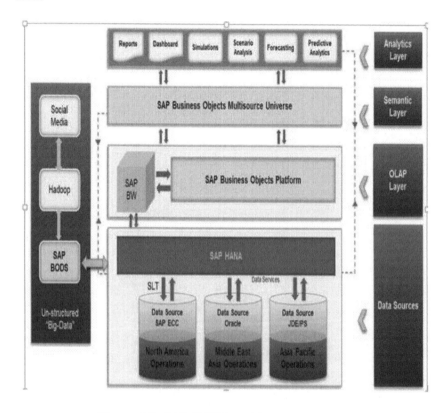

Figure 6.9 SAP HANA architecture overview

Image source: SAP AG / SE

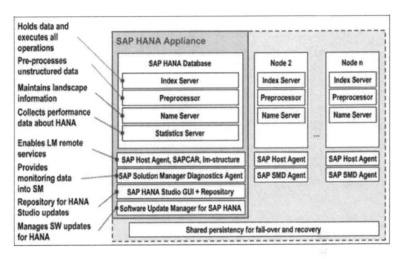

Figure 6.10   SAP HANA Core architecture overview

Image source: SAP AG / SE

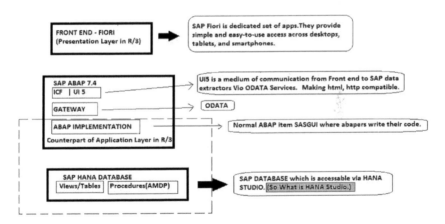

Figure 6.11 SAP HANA architecture

Image source: SAP AG / SE

Note: With Fiori, Customization of APP is possible. So, a dedicated user will see the APP which is dedicated to their Role.

An MM person who is authorized to Approve a PO will not be able to see the Sales order or Ledger balance. And in his mobile only MM things will be shown.

89. Explain an example of SAP R/3 or ECC architecture?

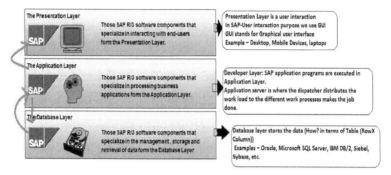

Figure 6.12 SAP R/3 architecture

Image source: SAP AG / SE

90. What are the differences between ECC and SAP HANA?

SAP ABAP / ECC	SAP HANA
Architecture difference (R/3) – 3 Tier architecture	In Memory DATA Base.
Accessibility: SAP GUI (Dedicated only for SAP)	Accessibility: ECLIPSE (ADT+ HANA Studio)
In Premises only.	– Multicore Processing/ Parallelism. (It's taking a Job and distributing among CPUs) – Massively Larger (3600 times proven faster) and cheaper in Memory. ON CLOUD or In- premises Deployment. (SPPED, Performance and Memory Capacity, Just an Awesome.)
Row Storage	– Columnar structure (better for retrieval performance. Already Sybase SY Q etc. are using this for 20 Years) – In Memory Computation. Code Push Down technique.(AMDP, CDS) - *ADBC Connection.

91. For SAP BW on SAP HANA what are the primary prerequisites?

Ans: Primary prerequisites

    a. Upgrade to SAP Net Weaver 7.02 or above

    b. Migrate database (RDBMS) to HANA DB

92. For SAP HANA, what is the operating system requirement?

Ans: SUSE Linux enterprise server

93. Via Scale up or Scale out configurations can SAP HANA server be configured?

Ans: Yes

94. Explain steps to implement standard Fiori apps?

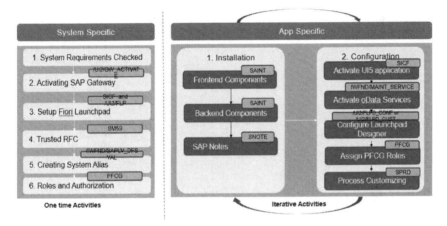

Figure 6.13 Standard Fiori apps implementation steps

Image source: SAP AG / SE

95. Explain typical Roles and Responsibilities in a Fiori Project?

Ans:

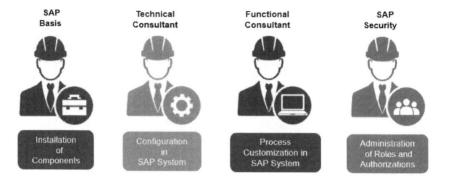

Figure 6.14 SAP S/4 HANA Fiori Roles

Image source: SAP AG / SE

96. Explain key concepts of SAP S/4 HANA?

Ans:

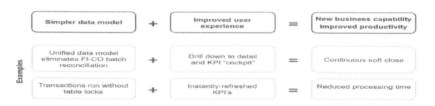

Figure 6.15 SAP S/4 HANA key concepts

Image source: SAP AG / SE

97. Explain how key innovations mapped to Product Map in SAP S/4
HANA?

Ans:

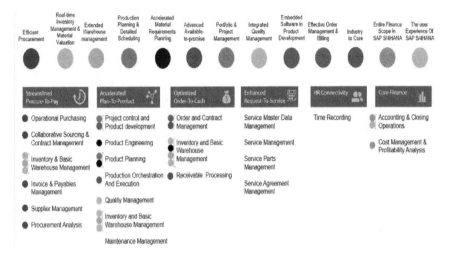

Figure 6.16 SAP S/4 HANA - Key Innovations mapped to Product Map
Image source: SAP AG / SE

98. Explain Data model simplification in SAP S/4 HANA?

Ans:

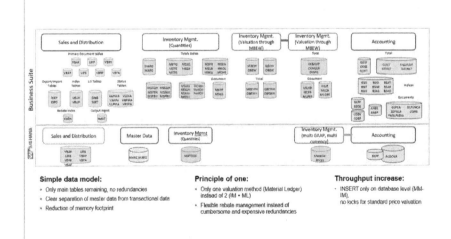

Figure 6.17 SAP S/4 HANA – Data Model Simplification
Image source: SAP AG / SE

99. Give an example of SAP Agile Team Members?

Ans:

- Regular cadence of meetings between SCRUM Masters of all SCRUM teams

- Goal is to coordinate and align work; highlight dependencies; discuss cross-topics

- SCRUM Masters have responsibility to debrief their respective teams on the results

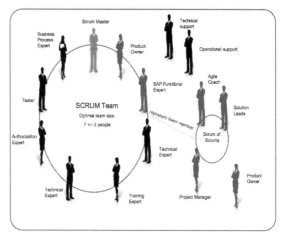

Figure 6.18 SAP Agile SCRUM Team overview

Image source: SAP AG / SE

100. Give example of "*Project Governance - In an Agile context*"?

Ans:

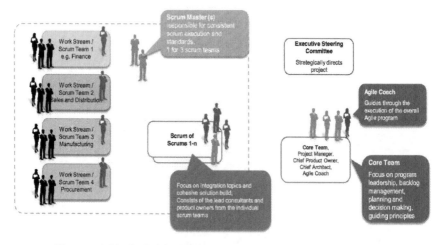

Figure 6.19 SAP S/4 HANA Project Governance overview

Image source: SAP AG / SE

101. Give an example of *"Day-to-Day Flow in SAP Agile Project"*?

Ans:

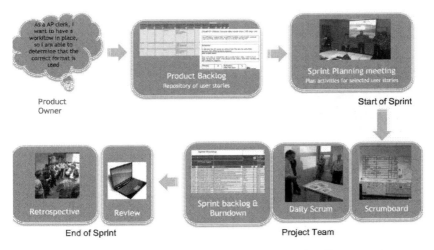

Figure 6.20 SAP S/4 HANA – Day to day flow

Image source: SAP AG / SE

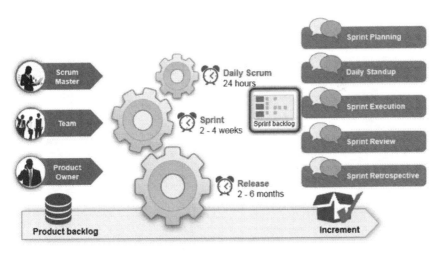

Figure 6.21 SAP S/4 HANA – SCRUM Ceremonies

Image source: SAP AG / SE

102. Give example of *"Validation and delta workshops in Explore phase"*?

Ans:

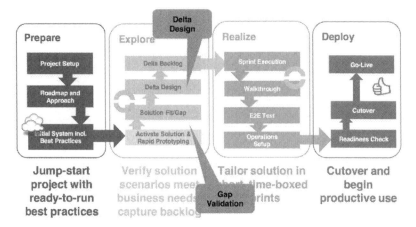

Figure 6.22 SAP S/4 HANA – Validation and delta workshops

Image source: SAP AG / SE

103. Give example of *"Supply-Chain-Planning Overview in S/4 HANA and SCM"*?

Ans:

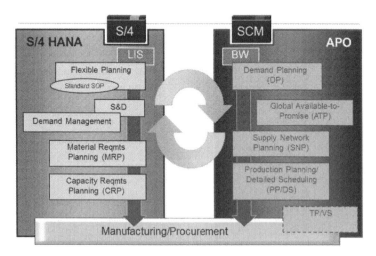

Figure 6.23 SAP S/4 HANA – Supply chain planning overview

Image source: SAP AG / SE

104. Give example of "*Sales Data Model Simplifications in S/4 HANA*"?

Ans:

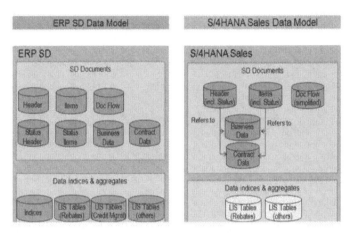

Figure 6.24 SAP S/4 HANA – Sales Data Model Simplification

Image source: SAP AG / SE

105. Give example of "Inventory Management – Data Model Redesign in S/4 HANA"?

Ans:

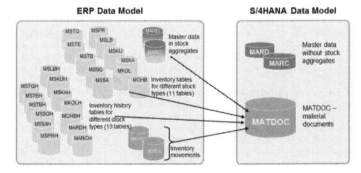

Figure 6.25 SAP S/4 HANA – Inventory Model Data Model Simplification

Image source: SAP AG / SE

Data Model simplification	Key Benefits
Merge material document header and item	Drop all aggregate fields and history tables (in total 24 tables)
Aggregated values for aged data as starting points	No updates on aggregation tables required anymore
Only one quantity column for all stock types	High speed evaluations
	Open for new stock types

106. Why users choose SAP S/4HANA in Enterprise Management?

Ans:

Figure 6.26 SAP S/4 HANA – Enterprise Management

Image source: SAP AG / SE

107. Explain "*S/4 HANA Conversion paths – from Business Suite to S/4 HANA*" ?

Ans:

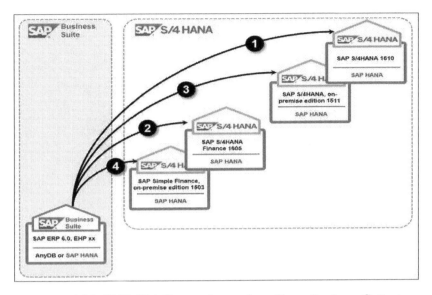

Figure 6.27 S/4HANA Conversion paths – From Business Suite to
S/4HANA

Image source: SAP AG / SE

	Start Release	Target Release	Availability	Remarks
1	SAP ECC 6.0 EHP 0-8	SAP S/4HANA 1610	available since: Q4/2016	Migration to SAP HANA DB [if required], Installation of S4CORE Software
2	SAP ECC 6.0 EHP 0-7	SAP S/4HANA Finance 1605	available since: Q2/2016	Migration to SAP HANA DB [if required], Installation of Software [**EHP8** + sFIN])
3	SAP ECC 6.0 EHP 0-7	SAP S/4HANA, on-premise edition 1511	available sinc : Q4/2015	Migration to SAP HANA DB [if required], Installation of S4CORE Software
	SAP ECC 6.0 **EHP8**	SAP S/4HANA, 1610	available since: Q4/2016	Migration to SAP HANA DB [if required], Installation of S4CORE Software
4	SAP ECC 6.0 EHP 0-7	SAP Simple Finance, on-premise edition 1503	available since: Q1/2015	Migration to SAP HANA DB [if required], Installation of Software [**EHP7** + sFIN])

Figure 6.28 S/4HANA Conversion paths overview
Image source: SAP AG / SE

108. Explain "*Transition to S/4HANA - System Conversion*"?

Ans:

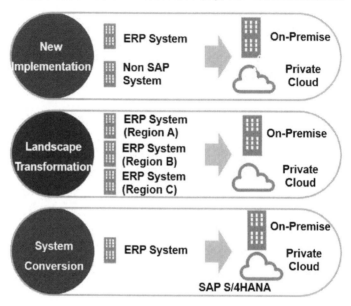

Figure 6.29 Transition to S/4HANA - System Conversion

Image source: SAP AG / SE

Figure 6.30 Transition to S/4HANA - System Conversion

Image source: SAP AG / SE

109. Explain "*S/4HANA Conversion paths – within S/4HANA domain*"?

Ans:

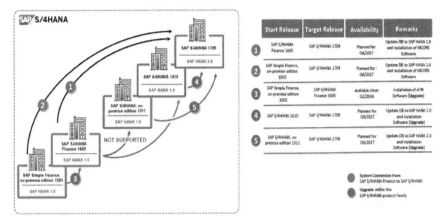

Figure 6.31 S/4HANA Conversion paths – Within S/4HANA domain

Image source – SAP AG / SE

110. Explain how the SAP Activate methodology guides teams implementing solutions in the public cloud?

Ans:

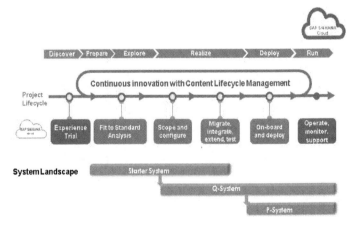

Figure 6.32 Overview System landscape in S/4 HANA Cloud Project

Image Source: SAP AG / SE

111. Explain the key deliverables per phase of S/4 HANA Activate methodology (Cloud)?

Ans:

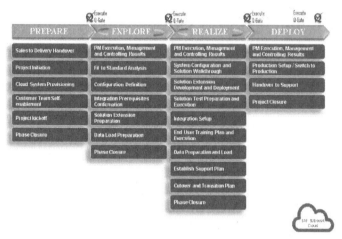

Figure 6.33 Key deliverables per phase of S/4HANA

Image source: SAP AG / SE

112. For new implementation of SAP S/4HANA cloud explain high-level summary users use to outline the approach?

Ans:

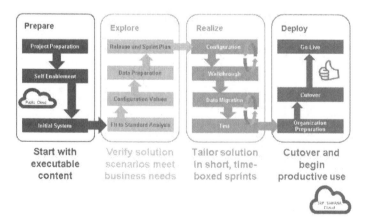

Figure 6.34 SAP S/4HANA Activate Phases overview

Image source: SAP AG / SE

113. Explain the key deliverables per phase of S/4 HANA Activate methodology (On-Premise)?

Ans:

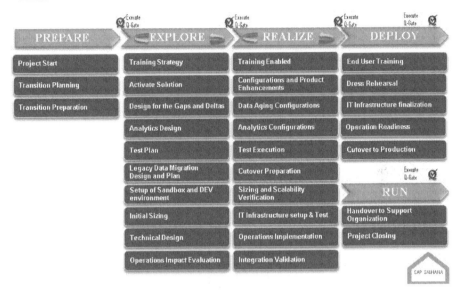

Figure 6.35 Key deliverables per phase of S/4 HANA Activate methodology

Image source: SAP AG / SE

114. *"Working Software is more important than documentation"*. Does it mean to produce no documentation at all?

Ans: *"Working Software is more important than documentation"*. But it does not mean to produce no documentation at all !

Keep it valuable, align with the organization perspective and agree solution documentation that is valued and can be maintained.

Solution documentation that is valued and maintained, is an INFORMATION ASSET for the organization.

The solution information assets will be stored in SAP solution manager.

115. Explain *"New Implementation differences: SAP Activate Versus ASAP 8 Implementation Methodologies"*?

Ans:

    a. Phase names are different in SAP Activate and in ASAP 8 Implementation Methodologies, SAP Activate has one less core phase.

    b. In SAP Activate, we are leveraging Agile during the project much more than in ASAP. SAP Activate defaults to an Agile iterative build with creation of a backlog of user stories.

However, in SAP Activate we emphasize the need for shorter cycles applying their mindsets of building, showing the customer how it is built and seeking the confirmation. This continuous cycle of building and validation is carried out throughout the entire project.

116. Explain *New Implementation similarities: SAP Activate Versus ASAP 8 Implementation Methodologies*?

Ans:

    a. WBS structure is Phase → Deliverable → Task

    b. Has option for an Agile or Waterfall project approach

    c. Testing activities have not changed equivalent phase (i.e., integration test, UAT and Performance test are all in REALIZE phase)

117. For new Implementations of SAP S/4 HANA is there any requirement to assemble and load SAP Best practices content?

Ans:

There is no requirement to assemble and load SAP Best practices content for new Implementations of SAP S/4 HANA because the system already contains the best practice content to be set in scope.

118. Explain Key Deliverables per Phase of JOURNEY New Implementation (On-Premise)?

Ans:

Figure 6.36 Key deliverables per Phase for new Implementation (On-Premise)?

Image source: SAP AG / SE

The figure serves as a reminder of the *Key Deliverables* per phase listed on the JAM site for a new implementation of an on-premise SAP solution.

This figure can also be used to help summarize the scope and discuss responsibilities for different parties in a project.

Note: Key deliverables often contain more than one individual deliverable (listed in the WBS).

Key Deliverables can span Workstreams (for example, where deliverables or tasks are associated with different Workstreams).

119. Explain one business scenario for System data migration?

Ans:

Business scenario: Customers who want to change their current system into SAP S/4 HANA system.

Database, NetWeaver, and Application transition in one step.

Customer benefits
- Migration without reimplementation
- No disruption for existing business
- Re-evalution of customization and existing process flows

Target audience

SAP Business Suite customers.

120. Explain Cutover preparation?

Ans:

All successful projects prepare well for their Cutover. The following activities have been done.
- Production system setup
- Create Cutover Plan (New Implementation)

Key deliverables
a. Data Migration and verification
b. Data Aging configuration

121. Explain handover to support organization?

Ans:

The project team will typically be involved in the initial post go-live support (sometimes referred to as *Hyper Care Support*) while the business and the support team get used to their new solution. The operations team will have been involved in the earlier project phases - and this handover to the support organization is one prerequisite for project closure.

The following tasks are performed here.
- Workload analysis
- Health check and scalability analysis
- Sizing verification
- Resolve and close open issues
- Handover operations responsibility

Key deliverables
a. Hyper care support
b. Handover to support organization.

122. Explain one example of new implementation?

Ans:

Example of new Implementation

New or existing SAP customers implementing a new SAP S/4 HANA system with initial data load.

Currently the majority of our customers are choosing the new implementation when they transition to SAP S4/HANA. This includes existing customers who use this scenario to re-think their processes and to take advantage of the simplified solution that SAP S/4HANA represents.

123. Explain one example of System conversion?

Ans:

Example of System conversion

Complete conversion of an existing SAP Business Suite system to SAP S/4 HANA.

In the system conversion case, the project teams are doing a series of migration and conversion activities as they go through the steps of moving the system from ECC6 on any DB to ECC6 on SAP HANA and then moving it into the SAP S/4HANA code base. All these activities are done through the SAP upgrade manager.

124. Explain one example of Landscape conversion?

Ans:

Example of landscape transformation

Consolidation of current regional SAP Business Suite landscape into one global SAP S/4HANA system.

It includes the consolidation of multiple systems into one system or carving out one company code to SAP S/4HANA.

125. Explain "Transition to SAP S/4HANA" - new Implementation scenario in a nutshell?

Ans:

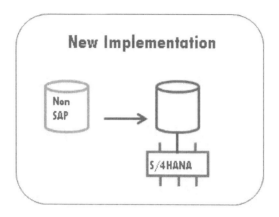

Figure 6.37 New implementation scenario in S/4HANA

Image Source: SAP SE / AG

126. Explain "Transition to SAP S/4HANA" - System conversion scenario in a nutshell?

Ans:

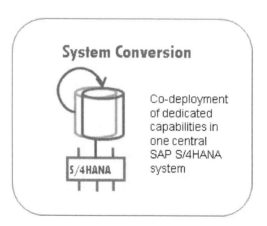

Figure 6.38 System conversion scenario in S/4HANA

Image Source: SAP SE / AG

127. Explain "Transition to SAP S/4HANA - landscape transformation scenario in a nutshell?

Ans:

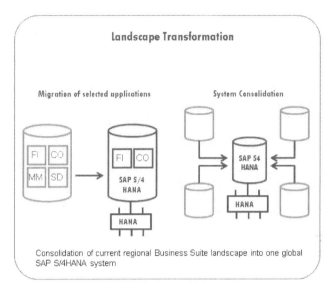

Figure 6.39 Landscape Transformation scenario in S/4HANA
Image Source: SAP SE / AG

128. Explain the key characteristics of the SAP Activate Implementation Approach?

Ans:

Key Characteristics of the SAP Activate Implementation Approach

a. **Start with best practices**: Use ready-to run business processes, on premise implementation, where we are leveraging the cloud appliance library to set up the sandbox system from a pre-configured best practice based software appliance.

b. **Validate solution**: Validate to best practices with fit/gap workshops, capture delta, to validate the solution fit, determine the delta requirements and capture gaps in the backlog list (instead of traditional blueprinting). In the Cloud implementations, there is a *fit-to-standard* approach where we identify configuration values to be set in the standard solution.

c. **Modular, scalable, and Agile**: Structure project to deliver the solution incrementally.

d. **Cloud Ready**: Leverage the flexibility and speed of the cloud.

e. **Premium engagement ready**: Build and run fully supported via SAP Control centers.

SAP offers services through premium engagements, such as SAP Active embedded or SAP max attention. These service offerings provide customers with access to control centers that help with activities like validation of perceived product gaps.

f. **Quality Built-in** Identify risk early with total quality approach. The SAP Activate methodology provides a structured approach for quality planning and quality management that has always been incorporated into SAP delivery methodologies.

129. What is the URL to access Roadmap Viewer tool?

Ans:

http://bit.ly/SAPRoadmapViewer

https://go.sap.corp/roadmapviewer

130. What is the URL to access SAP Jam site?

Ans: http://bit.ly/SAPActivate

131. What is the URL to access SAP Activate on sap.com?

Ans:

http://sap.com/activate

132. What is the URL to access SAP Service Marketplace?

Ans: http://service.sap.com/solutionpackages

133. What is the URL to access SAP S/4 HANA Trail Page?

Ans: http://www.sap.com/s4hana-trial

134. What is the URL to access SAP Best Practices Explorer?

Ans: http://rapid.sap.com/bp

135. What is the URL to access SAP Activate Cook-book?

Ans: https://go.sap.corp/cookbook

136. What is the URL to access Hybrid Integration Page?

Ans: http://service.sap.com/hybrid

137. Mention the two landscape transformation specific tasks in the explore phase?

Ans:

   a. Run a Landscape Transformation Assessment

   b. Setup Landscape Transformation Software

138. Mention the two landscape transformation specific tasks in the PREPARE phase?

Ans:

   a. Define the data migration architecture

   b. Transition Preparation

139. Mention the landscape transformation specific tasks in the REALIZE phase?

Ans:

   a. Perform Client Transfer (LT scenario – Client transfer)

   b. Perform Company code transfer (LT scenario – Company code transfer)

   c. Create Cutover Plan (Landscape transformation – Client transfer).

140. Explain one landscape transformation journey scenario in a nutshell?

Ans:

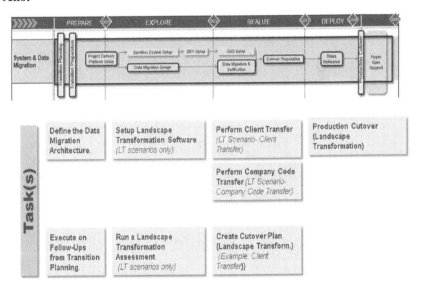

Figure 6.40 Landscape transformation scenario in S/4HANA

Image Source: SAP SE / AG

141. In how many ways can the Roadmap Viewer can be accessed?

Ans:

The Roadmap Viewer can be accessed from SAP methodologies Jam Site and SAP Solution Manager.

142. Define Roadmap Viewer?

Ans:

Roadmap viewer is a tool that gives access to a full work breakdown structure of a particular project type. The content is available in an on-line Fiori based environment.

It is hosted or managed within the ATP HANA Cloud platform. It shows the SAP Activate roadmaps for SAP S/4HANA and the SAP Activate roadmaps for other solutions.

Roadmap viewer allows customers and partners to view Solution Manager Roadmaps Online.

143. Name the three-level hierarchy of each roadmap?

Ans:

Each roadmap is a three-level hierarchy based on the SAP Activate methodology.

   a. Level 1: Phases

   b. Level 2: Deliverables

   c. Level 3: Task

144. Explain the key features of Roadmap Viewer?

Ans:

Key features:

- Roadmap Viewer allows customers and partners to view Solution Manager Roadmaps online

- Roadmap Viewer runs on the SAP S/4HANA Cloud Platform

145. How many ways you can navigate through the roadmap?

Ans:

You may navigate through the roadmap either using:

- Project phases
- Project work streams

146. How you can navigate via phases?

Ans:

Navigating via phase is done through selecting a specific phase (for example, Prepare, Explore, Realize, and Deploy).

147. How you can navigate via work streams?

Ans:

Navigation through workstreams is done by selecting a specific workstream; this then lists all the deliverables in that particular workstream.

148. Mention the deliverable in Roadmap Viewer?

Ans:

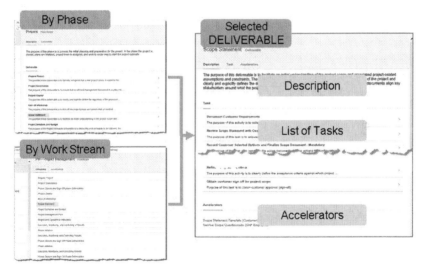

Figure 6.41 Roadmap Viewer deliverables overview
Image Source: SAP SE / AG

149. Mention the file formats when downloading a roadmap from the SAP Roadmap viewer?

Ans:

When downloading a roadmap from the SAP Roadmap viewer users receive a ZIP file with three different files/formats:

a. Spreadsheet

b. File to load to Microsoft Project

c. File to load to SAP Solution manager as a project

150. Why users need to check Roadmap Viewer regularly?

Ans:

Check into the Roadmap Viewer regularly because new or updated roadmaps are frequently published.

151. How many tiles are offered by SAP for Project Management?

Ans:

For Project Management there are three tiles which are offered by SAP:

a. My Projects

b. My Task

c. Project Analytics

152. What URL users need to refer for transaction support?

Ans:

For transaction support, users may refer URL: http://help.sap.com/ solutionmanager72

153. Why we need SAP Best practices for SAP S/4 HANA?

Ans:

We can increase value proposition and time-to-value with SAP Best practices.

SAP delivers a set of ready-to-run best practice processes with SAP S/4HANA.

SAP Best Practices provide the foundation for each implementation and give customers a jump start and reference solution from which to begin the implementation project.

In addition to these core, foundation SAP Best Practices, SAP delivers set of integration and migration best practices.

154. In the cloud what is the frequency to release new best practices?

Ans:

In the cloud, there are new best practices released with each release of the software (for example, every quarter).

155. In the SAP S/4HANA Cloud, on what Cloud Solutions SAP provides customers with best practices?

Ans:

In the SAP S/4HANA Cloud, SAP provides customers with best practices for each of the following Cloud Solutions:

- Enterprise Management
- Professional Services
- Marketing

156. What are the SAP Best Practices for SAP S/4HANA?

Ans:

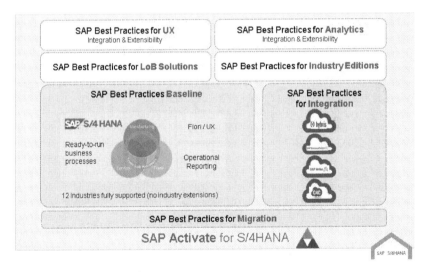

Figure 6.42 SAP Best Practices for SAP S/4HANA overview

Image Source: SAP SE / AG

Note: The figure for the on-premise edition is similar to that for cloud best practices, but contains additional items.

In addition to the ready-to-run business processes for SAP S/4HANA on-premise, the portfolio covers best practices for SAP Fiori and SAP UX. There are also best practices for operational reporting.

As with Cloud Best Practices the on-premise best practices are supported by Best Practices for data migration.

At the top of the figure we have a set of best practices for Line of Business solutions and Industry solutions. We recommend that you review the availability of these Best Practices across the SAP solution portfolio because the Best Practices are continually developed and expanded.

157. What are the benefits to accelerate Projects with Prebuilt Systems and Templates?

Ans:

a. Reduce time to value

b. More agility

c. Speed to innovation

d. Accelerate development and implementation

158. Explain the *Validate Solution* in cloud deployments and in an on-premise project?

Ans:

The *Validate Solution* characteristic is part of the EXPLORE phase.

In cloud deployments, this activity is referred to as fit-to-standard workshop. In the cloud, we emphasize the fit to the standard functionality in order to increase the ability to absorb the quarterly innovations that are provided in the cloud.

In an on-premise project the fit/gap has two types of workshops:

a. First is the solution validation workshops, where we validate the fit of the best practices to customer requirements. We refer to these workshops as Workshop A.

b. The second workshop is Delta design workshops in which the project team designs for the delta requirements and for the gaps.

159. Explain *Solution Validation workshop*?

Ans:

A Solution Validation workshop is not intended to educate participants. We recommend project teams to plan project team enablement and walkthroughs prior to these workshops to keep the workshop focus on the fit and gaps.

In these workshops the consultants will start with the overall solution before drilling down to process and function detail. Consultants will use the Best Practices documentation including the Business Process models to help facilitate the workshops.

The objective for the workshop is to challenge changes to standard functionality and determine if there is a need for changes or enhancements. Any changes need to be tied to business value or benefits.

The output of the solution validation workshop is a list of delta requirements and gaps.

160. Explain Delta Solution Design workshop?

Ans:

During this workshop, the team creates a design for addressing the delta requirements and resolving the gaps.

Customer business users have a key role in contributing during the design and acceptance of delta solution design.

Project team uses SAP Solution Manager as a toolset for solution documentation, including the delta design documents.

The methodology recommends the use of *Road Shows* to gain business acceptance, especially in larger projects.

161. Explain purpose of Fit/Gap Analysis?

Ans:

Purpose of Fit/Gap Analysis

The Fit/Gap Analysis has the following main objectives:

a. The primary objective is to have an updated and approved Scope Baseline to move into the Realization phase

b. Validate pre-activated or pre-assembled solution in the Sandbox system

c. Drive towards adopting SAP standard processes

d. Ensure that SAP implementation meets customer's business needs

e. Discover, clarify, and negotiate solution design

    f. Identify and capture delta business requirements and gaps (on top of the initial Sandbox system)

    g. Prioritize delta requirements and gaps

    h. Minimize the need for rework during Realization

162. Explain customer benefit of Fit/Gap Analysis?

Ans:

Accelerated time to value through content re-use, focus on differentiating capabilities.

163. Explain different steps of Fit/Gap Workshops?

Ans:

The figure provides further detail of what happens in each Fit/Gap Workshop.

In Step 1: Reference Value, consultants and key business users need to provide the strategic context, and value context based on the goals and objectives set for the project. This helps ground the discussion and set rules for the workshop. This includes setting the expectations and the boundaries for the workshop, so that the participants have a clear understanding of the purpose, format, and flow of the workshop as well as their role.

In Step 2: Validation of SAP Solution, the consultants walk the customer team through the sandbox system and demonstrate the standard process. During this step, consultants use the actual system as well as the best practices documentation. The customer looks at how the functionality appears in the system. The best practices come with a standard documentation of the business processes that will be showcased. We also show the business user roles involved in the process, and how the process flows.

In Step 3: Gap Identification, the team then captures any delta requirements and solution gaps in the backlog for future prioritization and delta design activities and places them into a backlog.

In Step 4: Backlog Prioritization, in between the workshops, the business users prioritize the backlog based on the desired sequence of the features to be implemented. This will set the sequence in which the project team conducts the delta design workshops and determines what they will focus on in the design sessions.

Workshop B has the focus on solutioning and design for the gaps and delta requirements.

In Step 5: Delta Design, the project team goes through the design activities, during which, for each priority delta requirement or gap, they update the Business Process Model, adjust the Business Processes Design, or define how to resolve a specific gap. As the team goes through the delta design, they may need to visualize some requirements and document, how the requirements will be implemented in the system.

Step 6: Verify and Accept, includes verification and acceptance at the end of the workshop B.

This is not a formal sign off for a blue print (like in ASAP). This step is a verification and acceptance of the backlog. The backlog is a living document in projects and we need to handle it as such.

In step 7, the project team conducts a detailed release and sprint planning for the Realize phase based on all the available information from the Explore phase and the Fit/Gap workshops.

Preparation for Workshops

Before the workshops, the team must prepare the system environment for Fit/Gap Analysis. This preparation includes doing the following:

a. Setup Initial System (Sandbox) based on SAP Best Practices, RDS, engineered services

b. Leverage pre-build solutions from SAP like SAP S/4HANA on-premise system in Cloud Appliance Library (http://cal.sap.com)

c. Add business data to the initial system

d. Extend the solution with some configuration for project scope not covered by SAP Best Practices (to support the workshop discussions)

e. Prepare release and sprint plan for Realize phase

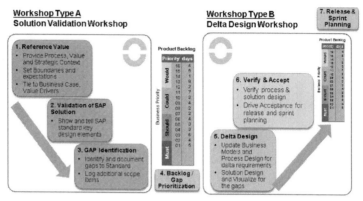

Figure 6.43 S/4HANA solution validation workshop

Image Source: SAP SE / AG

164. What are the key Components of Workshop A to Validate Solution?

Ans:

a. Reference / Set expectations

b. Review Process

c. Demo solution

165. What do you mean by Capture Delta Design Documentation?

Ans:

Create new process document for new processes leveraging agreed templates. Documentation on scenario and process level. For existing process adjustments (append existing documents, or update Business Process Design documents).

166. What do you mean by adjusting the Business Process Models?

Ans:

Create new process without disruption of global design, for example, P&L at plant level. As applicable, sub-processes can be created that tie into existing processes, for example, VAT which is common across multiple countries. Create a process variant for country, for example, Excise invoice generation as part of Billing. Leverage business process modeling tools. Use models delivered with Best Practices imported to SAP Solution Manager.

167. How do premium engagements help customers?

Ans:

Premium engagements are structured to help customers build their SAP Solutions in a factory like mode and run those solutions in factory like mode. Supporting aspects like the following:

a. Accelerating the implementation or accelerating time-to-value

b. Structuring the operations to support customer's goals within the IT organization and with the Business Reducing the implementation effort

c. Increasing the ability to innovate, by shifting the balance of the budget that the customer spends on IT management to business innovation

d. Lower project risk

e. Minimize total cost of ownership

168. Explain the benefits of build SAP like a factory?

Ans:

a. Accelerate time-to-value

b. Reduce total cost of implementation

c. Smoothen transition to operations

d. Support new business models

e. (Co-) Manage innovation

f. Prototype with LoBs

g. Adopt industry models best practices

169. Explain the benefits of run SAP like a factory?

Ans:

a. Improve business continuity

b. Higher degree of automation

c. Better business performance

d. Reduce total cost of operations

e. End user efficiency

f. Implement *Always Connected*

g. Simplify System Landscape

170. Explain the benefits of **Mission Control Center (MCC)?**

Ans:

a. Get access to the entire knowledge and experience of the SAP ecosystem

b. Ensure implementing best practices for solution operations

c. Risk mitigation during the project

d. Aligned with Value Advisory Center

e. Integrated with SAP Development

171. On what factors does the **Operations Control Center (OCC)** focus on?

Ans:

The **Operations Control Center (OCC)** focuses on the operations setup, including the zero downtime upgrades and business process improvement.

172. On what factors does the **Innovation Control Center (ICC)** focus on?

Ans:

The **Innovation Control Center (ICC)** services include Gap Validation and support for using content like Best Practices as well as support for integration validation.

173. What is the purpose of **Integration validation (IV)?**

Ans:

It ensures that the solution is scalable, data consistency is maintained, exceptions are identified and handled, custom code is optimized, interfaces throughput optimized, system parameter optimized, and the volume test represents true volumes.

174. How REALIZE phase is different in Agile project delivery compared to traditional waterfall projects?

Ans:

With an Agile project delivery, the way the Realize phase is run differs from traditional waterfall projects. The project team in SAP Activate uses an iterative, incremental approach that applies short cycles with customer feedback in each cycle. This model allows for more frequent feedback and continuous integration as the solution is being built. It also helps to structure the project into shorter and early cycles.

This is quite different from a traditional waterfall project, where we have the business participate in the blueprinting activities, then hand off the blueprint to the IT team to realize the functionality with minimal or no additional input from business until very late in the project. The business is brought back to participate in the user acceptance testing.

With SAP Activate, the business involvement is continuous and business users are involved in each iteration.

The project team will apply following principles in the solution build:

a. Introduce the Agile approach early, train the project team

b. Follow the standard Agile process, and apply the Agile principles

c. Focus the team on business priorities first by using the backlog prioritization

d. Frequent structured reviews with business users in each sprint

175. How does the 'Quality Built-In' characteristic help teams?

Ans:

The *Quality Built-In* characteristic helps teams identify risk early with a total quality view across the entire project. Quality Built-In is based on Quality Gates supported by SAP's ten principles of Quality with associated recordings.

176. Explain the four characteristics on which the 10 quality principles are based on?

Ans:

The recordings of the 10 quality principles are based on four distinct characteristics. These are as follows:

a. You need to understand how you can effectively follow the principles

b. Best Practices explaining how you can best manage the area covered by this principle.

c. The typical pitfalls that customers have experienced regarding this principle and that you may not be aware of.

d. Examples of the success factors that SAP customers who have won SAP Quality Awards have identified to achieve excellence in their implementation approach.

177. Explain the 10 quality principles for ensuring successful customer implementations in SAP Activate Methodology?

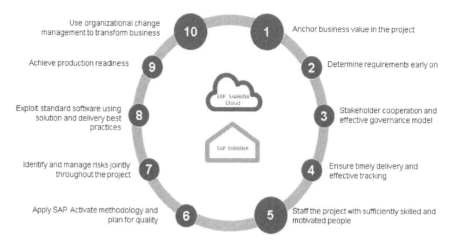

Figure 6.44

Image Source: SAP SE / AG

178. Mention the references for SAP quality principles?

1. Anchor business value firmly in your project: https://www.brainshark.com/sapgp/vu?pi=zGYzvBL0rz9yC3z0

2. Determine the requirements early on: https://www.brainshark.com/sapgp/vu?pi=zGuzUdDjUz9yC3z0

3. Cooperate with stakeholders and use a proper governance model: https://www.brainshark.com/sapgp/vu?pi=zG0zJXFQKz9yC3z0

4. Ensure timely delivery and effective tracking: https://www.brainshark.com/sapgp/vu?pi=zH3z18IqSNz9yC3z0

5. Staff the project with sufficiently skilled, motivated people: https://www.brainshark.com/sapgp/vu?pi=zG8zP6tJHz9yC3z0

6. Apply the appropriate methodology and plan for quality: https://www.brainshark.com/sapgp/vu?pi=zGXzWXPDbz9yC3z0

7. Identify and manage risks jointly throughout the project: https://www.brainshark.com/sapgp/vu?pi=zHjzawdEmz9yC3z0

8. Exploit standard software using solution and delivery best practices - https://www.brainshark.com/sapgp/vu?pi=zGmzDjY6wz9yC3z0

9. Achieve production readiness:https://www.brainshark.com/sapgp/vu?pi=zGqz7seCfz9yC3z0

10. Use organizational change management to transform business - https://www.brainshark.com/sapgp/vu?pi=zGlzTh5Iyz9yC3z0

11. Introduction to the Best Practices Series - https://www.brainshark.com/sapgp/vu?pi=zHXzZLmejz9yC3z0

12. Overview (PDF) : http://sapassets.edgesuite.net/sapcom/docs/2016/04/084bb1a5-6a7c-0010-82c7-eda71af511fa.pdf.

179. What is Quality gates in SAP Activate?

Ans:

Quality gates are built into the standard methodology. SAP places quality are the center of the project delivery.

A Quality Gate is a special milestone in a software project. Quality Gates are located before a phase that is strongly dependent on the outcome of a previous phase.

A Quality Gate provides oversight and early visibility into potential risks and issues. It has a profound impact on reducing risk and driving Customer Value.

Each Project Quality Gate verifies that the deliverable acceptance has been met and defines actions to support entry to the next project phase.

They are especially useful between phases in which breaches in disciplines must be overcome.

Quality gates can take a number of forms but in simplest terms they are a ... Management, quality gates are an inherent part of this process and part of the Project Management Plan.

180. What are the objectives of Quality gates in SAP Activate?

Ans:

a. Avoid customer dissatisfaction

b. Enable Project Managers to continuously communicate and build quality into the project

c. Assure quality at the milestones of the project

d. Assure that all key deliverables and actions have been completed in compliance with best practices

181. What are the benefits of Quality gates in SAP Activate?

a. Enhance project quality

    b. Minimize project risk exposure

    c. Manage expectations and monitor customer satisfaction

    d. Improve transparency of the project

    e. Reduce cycle time, get it done right the first time.

182. How many Quality Gates are mandated to perform for SAP implementation projects?

Four Quality Gates will be mandated to perform for SAP implementation projects.

183. Define phase in SAP Activate Methodology?

Phases are stages of the project. At the end of each phase, a quality gate exists to verify the completion of the deliverables.

184. Define workstream in SAP Activate Methodology?

A workstream is a collection of related deliverables that show the time relationships within a project and among the other streams. Streams can span phases and not necessarily dependent on phase starts and end.

185. Define deliverable in SAP Activate Methodology?

A deliverable is an outcomes that is delivered during the course of the project. Several deliverables are included within a workstream.

186. Define task in SAP Activate Methodology?

A task is work to be performed. One or several tasks comprise a deliverable.

Tasks represent the work or the activities that the project team performs. A group of tasks leads to the creation of the deliverable, which represents a tangible outcome that is handed over to the customer, or it may be an interim outcome in the context of the project.

187. What is the prime purpose of "Prepare phase" in SAP Activate Methodology?

In the Prepare phase, we perform activities that we have always performed at the beginning of a project. We define project governance, start the project, identify and define the resources, define the roles and responsibilities for the project team, and detail the management plans for running the project.

188. What is the prime purpose of "Explore phase" in SAP Activate Methodology?

In the Explore phase, we run the Fit/Gap analysis on the working system with the Best Practices content up and running. The objective of the Explore phase is to identify the fit of the best practices based solution, capture delta configuration requirements, identify gaps, and configuration values. All these are captured by the project team in the backlog. Later, in the Realize phase, the backlog items are implemented in the system. The best practices content is used as a jump-start for the project.

189. What is the prime purpose of "Realize phase" in SAP Activate Methodology?

During the Realize phase, the project team adopts an agile approach to iteratively and incrementally build the functionality from the backlog. This build follows the prioritization given by the product owner (for example, the business users) that continue to be involved with the project team during the sprints.

During the build, the team adds the configuration and development on top of the best practices content. Additionally, the team performs the unit and string testing during the sprints. In the Realize phase, the team also works on the integration of the overall solution to meet customer needs.

The Realize phase covers all the build and test activities required to prepare a release of functionality into production. This includes a full Integration test and user acceptance test before the team can continue into the Deploy phase.

190. What is the prime purpose of "Deploy phase" in SAP Activate Methodology?

The objective of the Deploy phase is to set up the production environment and confirm readiness to switch into business operations with the new solution. The team also performs sustainment and hyper-care activities in the Deploy phase once the system goes live.

Once the customer has switched over into the new environment, the project team helps the customer IT and business adopt and use the functionality. The team stay on-site for a pre-determined period of time, which is usually defined in the contract or agreed as part of the plan to transition to operations.

191. What is the purpose of discovery phase?
    a. Overall innovation strategy and roadmap creation
    b. Value and impact analysis
    c. Implementation strategy
    d. Technical architecture and infrastructure

192. What is the purpose of run phase?
    a. Application operations
    b. Business process monitoring
    c. ALM processes
    d. Optimization.

193. Name the deliverables of DISCOVERY phase?
    DISCOVERY phase deliverables include:
    a. Overall Innovation Strategy & Road Map Creation
    b. Value and Impact Analysis
    c. Implementation Strategy
    d. Technical Architecture & Infrastructure.

194. Name the accelerators in the Prepare phase?
    In the Prepare phase, we have different accelerators including the following:
    a. Delivery supplement
    b. Solution scope document
    c. Software and delivery requirements for the Best Practices
    d. Work Breakdown Structure
    e. And Project Management Plans and Governance documents.

195. Name the accelerators in the Explore phase?
    The Explore phase has more product specific content that the team leverages during the fit/gap analysis. These assets include the following:
    a. Customer presentation - A master deck that covers the scope of the solution and the service
    b. Master data overview - A table to understand the sample master data shipped in the package

    c. Organizational data overview - A table to understand the organization model data shipped in the package and how it relates to the software

    d. Process diagrams - A graphical representation of the steps in a scope item

    e. SAP Solution Manager template - A container for the implementation content for one or more solutions in an area that can be used in the SAP Solution Manager tool

    f. Project backlog template - Repository of all delta requirements and gaps to plan iterative, incremental build during Realize phase.

196. Name the accelerators in the Realize phase?

    a. Configuration guides

    b. Test scripts

    c. Methodology guidance for Agile approach, and

    d. The guides for cutover planning.

197. Name the accelerators in the DEPLOY phase?

    a. Project schedule

    b. Cutover plan

    c. Operations setup guide.

198. Name the accelerators that are delivered at the different layers of SAP Best Practices?

PFA the examples of accelerators that are delivered at the different layers.

    a. At the solution level, there are number of accelerators including presentations, content library link with access to all the best practices documentation, the administration guide, SAP Notes.

    b. At the scope item level, the SAP S/4HANA best practices deliver the fact sheet, which is the overview of the scope item with the description of the scope item, the business benefits, the business process model in BPMN notation, and the test scripts.

Activation of the best practices content by the project team is needed in the on-premise solution. In the cloud solutions, the best practices will be activated for the customer based on the input from the project team. The provisioned system will have the best practices pre-activated.

c. The building blocks come with the configuration guide document, which shows the detailed configuration settings for each building block. This document can be used as a reference if the configuration is used manually.

199. How to access SAP Best Practices Explorer?

In Q3 2016, the SAP Best Practices content was made available. (https://rapid.sap.com/bp/). This is a web channel experience to search, browse and consume SAP Best Practices and will replace the SAP Service Marketplace.

On the screen in the figure you can see there is a message when following the link to the SAP Best Practices Explorer suggesting that those accessing the link should sign-in with their SAP user Id (S-USER) to gain access to the detailed accelerators. For example this access is required to view the Configuration Guides relating to the Building Blocks.

The Best Practices packages can also be downloaded to SAP Solution Manager 7.2 within the Solution Administration (SOLADM) transaction.

Figure 6.45 S/4HANA On-Premise SAP best practices explorer

Image Source: SAP SE / AG

200. How to download SAP Best Practices content?

Before the Best Practices Explorer, and Best Practice content download to SAP Solution Manager 7.2, the Best Practices content was exclusively accessed through the SAP Service Marketplace.

The SAP Best Practices documentation, can be downloaded from SAP Service Marketplace. You can access the content on the page https://service.sap.com/rds and then go to the respective best practice package to download the documentation. We can access the download from here. Click the download button to download the documentation. In the SAP Service Marketplace, we have access to all the content including the fact sheets, software requirements, and additional details.

201. Why it is important in any project to have the standard definition of the Project Governance?

It is important in any project to have the standard definition of the Project Governance. It outlines the relationship between the different groups and stakeholders involved in the project.

The project governance describes the flow of information between the project and all the stakeholders. It specifies the decision making and escalation steps to resolve issues.

202. Explain the characteristics of the Project Governance framework?

The governance framework has a couple of characteristics that need to be established. It focuses on realizing the business value, managing the risk and issues, and enforcing the standards and accountability for the project.

It needs to be aligned with the governance that the organization already has in place. It also has to ensure that communication and messaging fits the organization and stakeholder needs. Governance needs to be adjusted to each customer. There is no one size that fits all.

The Project Manager establishing the governance needs to identify the key players who will be a part of the governance and then build in the stakeholder group. Generally the key players are specified within the project contract or Statement of Work (SoW).

The methodology provides recommendations for various project sizes - one example will be shown in the figure.

203. Explain the Project Governance Roles and Responsibilities?

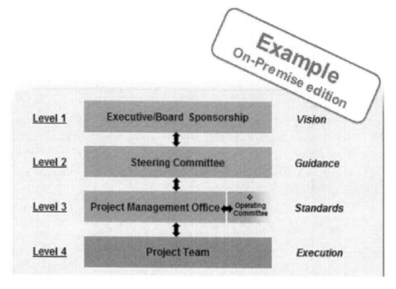

Figure 6.46 S/4HANA On-Premise edition example

Image Source: SAP SE / AG

The figure shows an example of the governance for on-premise project (medium to large size). In this example, there are four different levels.

At level 1, we have an Executive Sponsorship and level 2 covers the Steering committee. These two levels provide the project team with the vision and guidance. These levels also cover the setting of business priorities and overall strategy for the project.

On Level 3, you will find the Project Management Office comprising of the Project Manager and PMO staff. There is a link between the stakeholders of the project and the PMO. The PM plays a key role in interacting with the Steering group.

At Level 4 of the governance, we then find the project team that is performing the day-to-day execution of the project activities and are responsible for identification, resolution and communication of issues and risks to PMO. The PMO in turn then reports the key issues and key risks to the Steering Group and Executive Sponsor.

The governance establishes clear roles and responsibilities - for each governance level and project role.

204. Explain the Project Governance in an Agile Context?

In the context of an Agile project setup, we have a few roles that are shown in the figure. We have the project team structured into the scrum teams along the different work streams of the project.

Where the scrum master role is shared among the scrum teams, one scrum master can support up to three teams.

Another element for governing project execution in an Agile project is the scrum of scrums. These are typically weekly meeting in which the representatives of individual scrum teams meet to discuss any topics that are cross-team. In SAP projects, topics like cross-functional configuration, and the impact of functional settings on other teams are discussed. In some projects, people call these meeting an 'Integration Meeting'.

Additionally some agile teams procure services of an agile coach (either from SAP or an experienced coach from the industry) that helps the project manager, project teams, and leadership with various aspects of adopting the agile approach.

In addition, the PMO, Chief Product Owner and a Chief Architect oversee the overall project and solution.

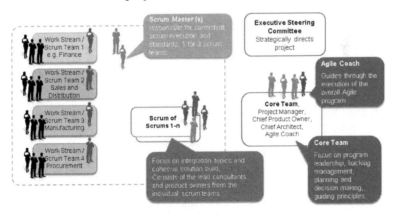

Figure 6.47 S/4HANA Activate Project Governance overview

Image Source: SAP SE / AG

205. Give a case study of SCRUM of SCRUMS?

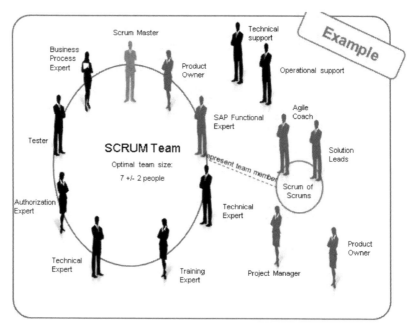

Figure 6.48 S/4HANA Scrum of Scrums Team

Image Source: SAP SE / AG

The project scrum teams are cross-functional. We have a product owner who works with the team. They can be the owner of single or multiple products. They coordinate the definition of the user stories (or requirements). When there are multiple product owners, we need to ensure that they all have clear accountability. In case of disagreement the decision may be addressed to the Chief Product Owner.

The project teams have one Scrum master assigned to the team, as well as a group of Business Process Experts, Testers, Authorization Experts, and Technical Experts. Some teams, in large projects, may have a dedicated authorization expert or even a developer if it is a large project. In a small project, some roles may be in the shared pool from which each scrum team borrows capacity of an expert in each sprint.

There will be differences in the composition of the scrum teams, but this is one example of how scrum team can be structured.

206. Give a high level comparison of Agile vs. DevOps?

Parameters	Agile	DevOps
Movement started	1993	2009
Focus	People (Customer, Employees)	Tools Automation
Scope	Business, development	Business, IT (Dev, QA) Operation, Security, infrastructure, Cloud, Networking, re-architecture
Outcome	Potentially shippable	Deploy, release, monitor Security, Stability, Reliability, Availability
Purpose	Servant Leader help (people, team)	End to end automation Help save dollars
For Coach Day-to-day	Mentor, coach, Trainer, facilitator	Consultant, Devops engineer Show by doing, make your hand dirty
Tries to answer	Are you working on right product? Is product usable? Are people (employee & customer) happy?	How fast can we scale up & down?

207. Explain digital transformation in a nutshell?

The digital transformation is the driver behind the fundamental changes that are taking place in society, the economy and industry. Typical factors are:

- New Internet-based technologies and applications
- SMACT – Social, Mobile, Analytics, Cloud, Internet of Things
- New communication and sales channels
- Changing customer behavior, "always on"
- Shorter product cycles
- Availability of real-time data
- Disruptive business models
- Creation of large volumes of unstructured data

- Advantages from the comprehensive analysis and evaluation of the data.

208. Explain the generic challenges faced by companies generally during digital transformation?

The challenges at a glance

The classic digitization challenges faced by companies and their IT staff are as follows:

- Rigid processes that prevent a fast response to changing requirements
- IT support and rapid implementation of new business models
- Complexity of reporting
- Problems during the analysis and evaluation of data
- Lack of integration and transparency of processes and data in the entire company
- Optimization of license management
- Simplification of system environments
- Consistency of systems and processes
- Avoidance of breaks
- Considerable demands on user experience by users and customers
- Outdated front ends and user interfaces
- Handling of customized developments and legacy applications
- Adequate use of conventional standards.

209. Explain SAP HANA advantages in a nutshell?

- Use of high-performance in-memory technology
- High-speed analysis and evaluation of very large volumes of unstructured data
- Ability to manage the exponentially growing data volumes resulting from the digitization process
- Acceleration of reporting and qualitative improvements in results
- Strategic business decisions based on sound insights

- Predictive analyses and reliable forecasts about future events
- Uniform view of information, doing away with data silos

210. Explain SAP S/4HANA advantages in a nutshell?

- Implementation of agile business processes to manage the digital transformation
- Process-spanning platform for consolidating and simplifying all processes in the company
- Consolidation of all relevant data and processes in one system
- Prevention of system breaks
- Opportunity for process-oriented work
- Reduction in coordination requirements, resulting in cost savings
- Flexible, customizable user interface
- Mobile, browser-based access to all applications, using a variety of devices
- Optional on-premise operation or flexible access through the cloud.

211. Explain SAP S/4HANA advantages in a nutshell?

- Implementation of agile business processes to manage the digital transformation
- Process-spanning platform for consolidating and simplifying all processes in the company
- Consolidation of all relevant data and processes in one system
- Prevention of system breaks
- Opportunity for process-oriented work
- Reduction in coordination requirements, resulting in cost savings
- Flexible, customizable user interface
- Mobile, browser-based access to all applications, using a variety of devices
- Optional on-premise operation or flexible access through the cloud.

212. How SAP HANA helps in Predictive analytics?

Predictive analytics

SAP HANA allows for predictive analyses. Now reliable forecasts may be made about future events based on the analysis of large data volumes in real time. This results in many possible applications for marketing and sales purposes. One example: when visiting a website, users leave information about their interests and product preferences. This data offers a lot of potential. If it is comprehensively analyzed, companies can calculate probabilities about which products users will buy in the future. Now the provider can not only keep certain items in stock, but also design products according to the specific requests of their client base in the future.

213. Explain SAP HANA in a nutshell?

With the introduction of HANA (High Performance Analytic Appliance) in 2010, SAP was the first provider to offer a development platform for software applications with databases based on in-memory technology. In contrast to conventional databases, the platform uses the computer's RAM – and not the hard drive – to store data. The CPU can access this memory much faster than the hard drive, resulting in the enormous speed of in-memory technology. It means that compared to relational database applications, these solutions can be used to search through, analyze and evaluate very large volumes of unstructured data (big data) with better performance and virtually in real time.

Another factor is that all internal and external data is now contained in one single database. This speed gives rise to the many advantages offered by SAP HANA. Thanks to the considerable analysis performance, relevant information and insights can be quickly extracted from big data, which the company can use to its advantage. Thus SAP HANA is the ideal technology for successfully managing the enormous data volumes resulting from the digitization process.

Now reporting can be accelerated, and the quality of the results is also significantly improved. In this way, management is able to make the correct disruptive business decisions on the basis of sound insights.

214. Explain SAP S/4HANA in a nutshell?

SAP S/4HANA may be viewed as the consistent enhancement of SAP HANA. Based on the superior in-memory database technology,

SAP introduced S/4HANA in 2015, a comprehensive next-generation real-time ERP suite. The product suite paves the way to immediate digital creation of value in all business divisions and at companies of all industries and sizes. SAP S/4HANA is designed in such a way that it can be operated on an on-premise basis at the company or through the Cloud. Using the apps from the SAP Fiori product line, users can personalize their user interface and flexibly access applications through a variety of devices such as smartphones and tablets.

The great advantage of SAP S/4HANA is the process-spanning platform which channels, consolidates and simplifies all of the processes in the company. While traditional ERP systems often file redundant documents and other data, SAP S/4HANA uses a centralized storage system. This prevents breaks and provides users with an overview of the entire process, enabling them to work in a process-oriented rather than transaction-related manner – as is the case with conventional ERP solutions.

215. How SAP S/4HANA helps in reducing coordination requirements in financial accounting?

One example: in financial accounting and controlling, the use of centrally stored documents can significantly reduce coordination requirements, resulting in cost savings. Direct access to source documents also offers considerable flexibility for the preparation of queries, which means that, for example new business ideas can now be analyzed more quickly. In addition, users benefit from the flexible and customizable graphical user interface (GUI). They can now use a conventional Internet browser to access all applications, independent of device and location. In this way, SAP S/4HANA can be used to implement agile business processes for managing the digital transformation.

216. Explain the concerns/issues/road blockers regarding implementation of SAP HANA and SAP S/4HANA?

Many companies have long recognized the numerous advantages offered by SAP HANA and SAP S/4HANA and have put the implementation of such systems on their to-do lists. This is also confirmed by the results from the previously mentioned study conducted by Pierre Audoin Consultants in 2015. Nevertheless, IT managers and decision-makers still have concerns regarding the implementation of SAP HANA or SAP S/4HANA. In the PAC study,

78 percent of companies surveyed indicated that the requirements for migrating to SAP S/4HANA are difficult to estimate. A similar percentage of study participants complained about the lack of business cases needed to justify the required investments. And 76 percent of those surveyed believe that the costs for new software licenses are simply too high.

217. Explain the criteria for successful implementation of SAP HANA and SAP S/4HANA in a nutshell?

How can companies do away with these concerns and benefit from SAP HANA or SAP S/4HANA without restrictions? First of all, they must consider whether a complete migration to SAP HANA or SAP S/4HANA is even required at this time. It is possible that it would make more sense, given the current conditions, to gradually get the departments involved ready for the digital transformation, for example by outsourcing certain processes or migrating an existing business management system to SAP HANA. This can be followed by additional measures in the direction of digital process optimization.

It is only at the next step that companies must ask themselves how the systems can be introduced professionally, with a high probability of success and reasonable efforts and costs. IT managers are well advised to use an approach consisting of careful planning, well-thought-out strategies and gradual implementation:

Step 1: Performing a process analysis

Step 2: Defining objectives

Step 3: Defining a strategy

Step 4: Developing a road map.

218. Explain the process to do a process analysis of any SAP HANA or SAP S/4HANA implementation project in a nutshell?

A sound analysis of the existing business processes at the company should be the starting point of any SAP HANA or SAP S/4HANA implementation project. Therefore the status quo must be determined on the basis of the following questions:

- What exactly are the internal processes in the business?
- How are they implemented in practice?
- What bottlenecks/difficulties arise?

- Do the employees even recognize them as such? Or have temporary solutions already become routine?
- Which types of risks arise daily due to process errors?

It is important that the stock-taking process is honest and comprehensive, for example in the form of audits with managing employees and supported by process mining tools. In this way, the status quo can not only be analyzed but also visualized.

Additional factors must also be considered:

- Release status of the SAP systems
- Code structure of existing database systems
- Status of the operating systems and applications, e.g. MS Windows
- What types of in-house developments are there?
- Does the company work with an old or new general ledger?

219. Explain the process of defining objectives of any SAP HANA or SAP S/4HANA implementation project in a nutshell?

The second step defines the destination of the journey: using the problems identified in the first step, it must now be discussed where the potential for improvement lies and what the ideal target state that is to be achieved with the introduction of SAP HANA or SAP S/4HANA, looks like. Which key performance indicators can be used to measure the desired successful outcomes?

The definition of targets also requires precise deadlines: by what date should the introduction of SAP HANA or SAP S/4HANA be completed? And by when should the corresponding process improvements take effect?

220. Explain the process of defining a strategy of any SAP HANA or SAP S/4HANA implementation project in a nutshell?

Once your Project objectives and scope is clear, organization must set up strategy for benefits realization & outcome measurement. Continuously inspect, adapt, and based on customer feedback continuously work upon process improvements using SAP HANA or SAP S/4HANA and consistently aligning them to the defined objectives.

221. Explain the process to develop a roadmap of any SAP HANA or SAP S/4HANA implementation project in a nutshell?

Once the strategic deliberations have been completed, it is possible to develop a concrete road map that describes the various implementation steps. This requires the definition of clear deadlines, hence a chronology of the intended progress of the project, such as specific information as to when e.g. the analysis phase must be completed, which preparatory activities are required (e.g. data migrations), when can the implementation begin and by what date are the improved processes supposed to take effect.

222. Under "Consumer" industry cluster what are the specific industries SAP S/4HANA supports?

- Consumer Products
- Wholesale
- Life Science
- Retail including fashion and vertical business.

223. Under "Discrete" industry cluster what are the specific industries SAP S/4HANA supports?

- Aerospace & Defense
- High Tech
- Industrial Machinery and Components
- Automotive

224. Under "Energy & Resources" industry cluster what are the specific industries SAP S/4HANA supports?

- Chemicals
- Mining
- Mill Products
- Utilities

225. Under "Financial Services" industry cluster what are the specific industries SAP S/4HANA supports?

- Banking
- Insurance

226. Under "Public Services" industry cluster what are the specific industries SAP S/4HANA supports?

- PS & Postal

227. Under "Services" industry cluster what are the specific industries SAP S/4HANA supports?

- Engineering, Construction, and Operations
- Professional Services
- Telecommunications.

228. Explain the use of "Structuring Technical Objects Hierarchically and Horizontally" in a nutshell in SAP S/4HANA?

The functional location is an organizational unit that structures the maintenance objects of a company according to functional or process-related criteria. When creating a functional location and defining its place in the hierarchical structure you define where a piece of equipment can be installed. Pieces of equipment can be installed in different functional locations or in other pieces of equipment.

As functional locations represent your company's operational structures, they are usually part of a hierarchical structure and you can summarize costs or other maintenance data for individual hierarchy levels. Based on the structure indicator, functional locations are automatically arranged in the structure when you create them. You can also create hierarchical equipment structures if you want to divide large pieces of equipment into smaller units.

If you want to structure your technical systems horizontally, you can create object networks. Object networks are represented by links between various pieces of equipment or functional locations.

229. Explain the use of "Creating Master Records for Functional Locations and Pieces of Equipment" in a nutshell in SAP S/4HANA?

Once the structure of the asset is defined, you can create a master record for each functional location and piece of equipment and specify general data, location data, organizational data, and structure data as well as edit classification data and characteristic values, and assign documents.

- You can assign a bill of material (BOM) to the master record of a functional location or piece of equipment.

- After having created characteristics and classes, you can assign this classification information to the master records of equipment and functional locations. If you have to manage a large number of objects, the classification enables you to easily locate your objects and group them together for evaluations.

- You can serialize a piece of equipment by assigning a material number and serial number to it. This makes inventory management possible for the equipment.

- A piece of equipment that is installed in a technical object can store the history of its installation location. The system records a usage period for each installation location, enabling you to track the complete installation history.

- In the equipment master record uou can maintain fleet information, such as data pertaining to the engine and fuel.

  Users can represent objects that are not repaired but rather exchanged in case of a breakdown by creating master records for materials and assemblies. Although this does not enable you to document a maintenance history, a material or assembly can also serve as a reference object for a maintenance notification or order.

230. Explain the use of "Creating Maintenance Bills of Materials (BOMs)" in a nutshell in SAP S/4HANA?

A maintenance bill of material (BOM) is a complete, formally structured list of the components making up a technical object or an assembly. Maintenance BOMs support you when locating malfunctions by providing you with an overview of all components that make up a technical object. From this overview you can easily select the object for which you want to create a malfunction report. Furthermore, maintenance BOMs provide you with an overview of all spare parts used for the maintenance of a specific technical object, so they make spares planning considerably easier.

A maintenance BOM contains the object numbers of the individual components together with their quantity and unit of measure, and can be assigned to the master record of a technical object or material.

231. Explain the use of "Master Data" of asset master in a nutshell in SAP S/4HANA?

Asset master record may be used to create, edit, and manage the master data of Asset Accounting.

232. Explain the use of "Asset Acquisitions and Asset Retirements" in a nutshell in SAP S/4HANA?

You can post asset acquisitions integrated with accounts payable accounting or not integrated.

Similarly, you can post asset retirements integrated with accounts receivable accounting or not integrated.

In addition to this, there are more functions available for asset acquisitions and retirements.

233. Explain the use of "Depreciation" in a nutshell in SAP S/4HANA?

With depreciation you map impairments incurred or impairments that are due to tax law requirements.

234. Explain the use of "More Transactions, Reversal" in a nutshell in SAP S/4HANA?

More transactions, for example post-capitalizations are available.

You can reverse documents that are posted in Asset Accounting.

231. Explain the use of "Postings and Documents" in a nutshell in SAP S/4HANA?

Asset Accounting is based on the universal journal entry. General Ledger Accounting and Asset Accounting are therefore reconciled per se; this means that reconciliation postings are not necessary as part of closing operations.

235. Explain the use of "Closing Operations and Reporting" in a nutshell in SAP S/4HANA?

You post the depreciation amounts periodically, directly in General Ledger Accounting.

Create an asset history sheet to represent the development of the fixed asset from the opening balance through to the closing balance.

More tools for the reporting and analysis of asset portfolios, asset transactions, and depreciation (including depreciation forecast and simulation) are also available.

236. Explain the use of "Parallel Accounting" in a nutshell in SAP S/4HANA?

You can manage Asset Accounting in accordance with several accounting principles simultaneously, for example with a local accounting principle and the accounting principle of a corporate group. This happens in the same way as in General Ledger Accounting. Separate documents are posted for each accounting principle.

237. Explain the use of "Identify contracts" in a nutshell in SAP S/4HANA?

You can create revenue accounting contracts corresponding to orders, contracts, bills or invoices, meaning revenue documents, that are created on an operational system, such as Sales and Distribution or third-party systems.

238. Explain the use of "Allocate the transaction price" in a nutshell in SAP S/4HANA?

You can determine the total price by aggregating the pricing conditions and then allocate the total price among the performance obligations.

239. Explain the use of "Manage the fulfillment of performance obligations" in a nutshell in SAP S/4HANA?

You can recognize revenue for performance obligations as they are fulfilled either at a point in time or over time.

240. Explain the use of "Make revenue postings" in a nutshell in SAP S/4HANA?

You calculate contract liability and contract asset values and make postings to the general ledger to reflect revenue-related recognition transactions.

241. Explain the use of "Automatic Valuation of Material Inventories" in a nutshell in SAP S/4HANA?

Valuation of material inventories in multiple currencies in parallel.

242. Explain the use of "Optional Price Controls for Materials" in a nutshell in SAP S/4HANA?

Perpetual valuation of material inventories and movements at standard cost or moving average.

243. Explain the use of "High Throughput of Logistics Data" in a nutshell in SAP S/4HANA?

Manage high logistics data volume.

244. Explain the use of "Manual Adjustments to Material Costs and Inventory Values" in a nutshell in SAP S/4HANA?

Adjust material costs and inventory values manually.

245. Explain the use of "Periodic Valuation of Material Inventories" in a nutshell in SAP S/4HANA?

According to statutory or product cost management requirements doing valuation of material inventories .

246. Explain the use of "Analyze Inventory Values" in a nutshell in SAP S/4HANA?

Real-time line item reports aggregated to inventory positions on the fly, with drill-down capabilities.

247. Explain the use of "Import of supplier invoices" in a nutshell in SAP S/4HANA?

You use this feature to import multiple supplier invoices all at once.

248. Explain the use of "Analysis of payments to suppliers" in a nutshell in SAP S/4HANA?

You use this feature to view information about payments to suppliers. Checking the overdue payable amount and the future payable amount is possible.

You can notify the responsible persons to take action in case if you identify negative trends in the payable amount.

249. Explain the use of "Management of cash discounts" in a nutshell in SAP S/4HANA?

Forecasting the available cash discounts and to monitor the cash discount utilization in your responsible area is possible.

In order to avoid cash discount loss in the future you need to find out where you need to make better use of cash discounts.

250. Explain the use of "Reviewing of cleared overdue invoices" in a nutshell in SAP S/4HANA?

Getting details and statistical facts about cleared overdue invoices is possible by utilizing this feature.

251. Explain the use of "Evaluation of days payable outstanding" in a nutshell in SAP S/4HANA?

You use this feature to identify suppliers with the highest or the lowest days payable outstanding.

252. Explain the use of "Management of payments" in a nutshell in SAP S/4HANA?

    You use this feature to create, post, and, if necessary, reverse payments.

253. Explain the use of "Management of payment blocks" in a nutshell in SAP S/4HANA?

    You use this feature to set and remove payment blocks on invoices or supplier accounts. You can identify irregularities or potential fraud in invoices through integration with SAP Fraud Management for SAP S/4HANA*.

254. Explain the use of "Management of payment proposals" in a nutshell in SAP S/4HANA?

    You use this feature to revise and release payment proposals. Journal entries are then generated in the finance system.

255. Explain the use of "Management of payment media" in a nutshell in SAP S/4HANA?

    You use this feature to transfer the data required for electronic payment transactions to banks via a data medium. A payment medium is created with each successful payment run.

256. Explain the use of "Posting Business Transactions" in a nutshell in SAP S/4HANA?

    You can post accounting data for customers in accounts receivables and the data entered is transferred to the general ledger. General ledger accounts are updated according to the transaction concerned (receivable, down payment, bill of exchange, and so on).

257. Explain the use of "Clearing of Open Invoices" in a nutshell in SAP S/4HANA?

    You can post incoming payments and either manually clear open items or have them cleared automatically by the system.

258. Explain the use of "Periodic Activities and Closing Operations" in a nutshell in SAP S/4HANA?

You can prepare and carry out periodic activities, such as automatic payment or dunning, or activities that arise for day-end closing, month-end closing or year-end closing.

259. Explain the key features in a nutshell during financial closing operations?

Key Features

Generally, financial closing operations include the following tasks:

- Maintain exchange rates
- Execute recurring entries
- Clear open items
- Perform inventory and post inventory differences
- Reclassify clearing account for goods receipt/invoice receipt
- Valuate materials
- Perform closing operations in the subsidiary ledgers
- Perform foreign currency valuation
- Reclassify receivables and payables
- Use functions for tax on sales/purchases
- Perform reconciliation between affiliated companies; these intercompany reconciliations are used in preparation for consolidation.
- Close posting period and open new posting period
- Display financial statements
- Execute balance carryforward
- Evaluate financial statements.

260. Explain the use of "Data Collection" in a nutshell in SAP S/4HANA?

You can collect individual financial statement data from SAP systems as well as non-SAP systems. Various procedures are available for doing this.

261. Explain the use of "Data Validation" in a nutshell in SAP S/4HANA?

You can define validation rules and assign the rules to various dimension combinations to verify the data quality before releasing data for consolidation use.

262. Explain the use of "Modeling" in a nutshell in SAP S/4HANA?

The Model can be used to bundle all of the characters and key figure definitions, customizations, and putting final consolidated results into a separate consolidation context. You use the modeling process to decide which fields are needed for consolidation dimensions, and which are needed to join with global settings to form the data basis for consolidation.

263. Explain the use of "Analysis of payments to suppliers" in a nutshell in SAP S/4HANA?

Viewing information about payments to suppliers is possible.

Another possibility is to check the overdue payable amount and the future payable amount.

You can notify the responsible persons to take appropriate corrective action and preventive action in case if you identify negative trends in the payable amount.

264. Explain the use of "Management of cash discounts" in a nutshell in SAP S/4HANA?

Forecasting the available cash discounts and monitoring the cash discount utilization in your responsible area can be done by using this feature.

In order to avoid cash discount loss in the future you can find out where you need to make better use of cash discounts.

265. Explain the use of "Reviewing of cleared overdue invoices" in a nutshell in SAP S/4HANA?

Getting details and statistical facts about cleared overdue invoices are possible by using this feature.

266. Explain the use of "Evaluation of days' payable outstanding" in a nutshell in SAP S/4HANA?

Identification of suppliers with the highest or the lowest days' payable outstanding can be done by using this feature.

267. Explain the use of "Management of payment media" in a nutshell in SAP S/4HANA?

You use this feature to transfer the data required for electronic payment transactions to banks via a data medium. A payment medium is created with each successful payment run.

268. Explain the use of "Management of payment blocks" in a nutshell in SAP S/4HANA?

Setting and removing payment blocks on invoices or supplier accounts can be done by using this feature.

You can identify irregularities or potential fraud in invoices through integration with SAP Fraud Management for SAP S/4HANA*.

269. Explain the use of "Posting Business Transactions" in a nutshell in SAP S/4HANA?

Posting of accounting data for customers in accounts receivables can be done and the data entered is transferred to the General Ledger (GL). GL accounts are updated according to transactions involved (like, Receivable, Downpayment, Bill-of-exchange, and so on).

270. Explain the use of "Correspondence" in a nutshell in SAP S/4HANA?

You can send correspondence to your customers, such as payment notices, open item lists, balance confirmation or account statements. You can adjust the forms for the correspondence according to your requirements.

271. What is the intelligent enterprise, and why should I care?

Technologies such as artificial intelligence, the Internet of Things, machine learning, and advanced analytics are creating major competitive advantages for businesses. But not on their own. By reimagining the future and adopting these technologies to help make sense of their large volumes of data, organizations will gain both strategic and tactical advantages.

Intelligent use of data and applications can help organizations predict the future far more accurately and identify opportunities earlier. They can also help:

- Provide an optimal customer experience to drive ongoing loyalty
- Improve productivity through more efficient business and supply chain operations
- Improve the skill and increase the engagement of your entire workforce

This is your watershed moment – one that has the power to change your operating practices for the better and for good. So, there's no time like the present to let SAP help you lay your foundation for the future.

272. After Project creation when it is recommended to conduct Project kick-off meeting?

Conduct Project kick-off meeting within 2 weeks of Project creation.

273. What is the Project Management Review (PMR) frequency based on Project Criticality index?

Project Criticality Index	PMR Frequency
Low	Atleast once in quarter
Medium	Atleast once in quarter
High	Monthly

274. Give an example of FMEA?

FMEA (Failure Mode and Effects Analysis) example - This technique can be used to ensure a robust design by focusing on potential failure modes associated with the functions of a system caused by design.

275. Name different XP practices?

XP 12 Practices

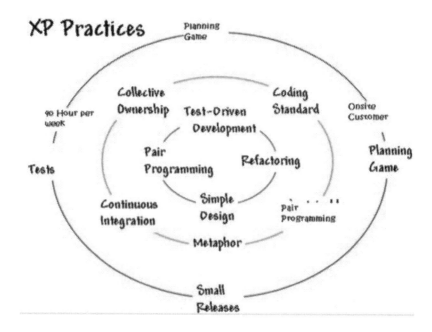

    a. The Planning Game

    b. Small Releases

    c. Metaphor

    d. Simple Design

    e. Testing

    f. Refactoring

    g. Pair Programming

    h. Collective ownership

    i. Continuous integration

    j. 40-hour week

    k. On-site customer

    l. Coding standards.

276. Explain Greenfield Programs in a nutshell?

They provide the facilities which are installed and commissioned right from scratch including software, networks and infrastructure.

277. Explain Brownfield Programs in a nutshell?

Brownfield Programs provide those facilities, which are modified / upgraded from existing (legacy) software applications / systems, are called Brownfield Programs. Example, system conversion.

278. What is a Gap?

A **gap** is defined as any transaction that cannot be processed in the system as it is currently configured.

What will SMEs be asked to do in the Fit-Gap sessions?

1. **Assess** the standard solution proposed for relevant Federal Integrated Business Framework-defined capabilities and Customer unique mission business needs

2. **Validate** that the standard solution meets business needs

3. **Identify gaps** and **complete the Customer Response Forms** during and after the session

4. **Submit to Provider** for collection; SMEs should submit their Response Forms within 5 days after the last session that they attend

279. How will the gap be dispositioned?

    - Collect and consolidate gaps from Customer Response Forms into Gap Tracker
    - Share Gap Tracker with Program Advisors for validation
    - Obtain gap validation and disposition from Program Advisors within 10 days after the session
    - Consolidate and publish on SharePoint final list of gaps and disposition obtained from Program Advisors.

280. How will the gap be dispositioned?

    - Collect and consolidate gaps from Customer Response Forms into Gap Tracker
    - Share Gap Tracker with Program Advisors for validation
    - Obtain gap validation and disposition from Program Advisors within 10 days after the session
    - Consolidate and publish on SharePoint final list of gaps and disposition obtained from Program Advisors.

281. Generally, what is the frequency to submit Metrics?

    Monthly.

282. Explain the use of "Accruals processing" in a nutshell in SAP S/4HANA?

    Posting accruals based on relevant invoices to update the bonus entitlements for future customer or supplier settlements in accounting.

283. Explain the use of "Archiving" in a nutshell in SAP S/4HANA?

    Archiving of documents to remove volumes of data from the database that are no longer required in the system, but still need to be kept for analysis purposes.

284. In "Discrete Manufacturing" how you convert planned orders into production orders or process orders?

    You can convert planned orders for materials that are to be produced in-house to production orders. You can convert your planned orders manually or automatically using an order conversion run. The material components required for production are contained as items in the planned order and are copied to the production order. The dependent requirements for the components are converted into reservations.

With the conversion to production orders, the responsibility is passed on from the MRP controller to the production supervisor.

285. In "Process Industry" how you convert planned orders into production orders or process orders?

In this case, you convert planned orders into process orders. Again, you can convert your planned orders manually or automatically using an order conversion run. The material to be produced, the order quantity, and the order dates are copied from the planned order to the process order and the dependent requirements for the components are converted into reservations. With the conversion to process orders, the responsibility is passed on from the MRP controller to the production supervisor.

286. In "Repetitive Manufacturing" how you convert planned orders into production orders or process orders?

In repetitive manufacturing, planned orders can be used to trigger production. In this case, the planned orders do not have to be converted into production or process orders.

287. Explain the use of "Picking" in a nutshell in SAP S/4HANA?

You can use the picking function to determine which components have not yet been issued from stock for an order and then you can perform the goods issue.

288. Explain "Make-to-stock production" in a nutshell in SAP S/4HANA?

Production is controlled without a direct reference to the sales order. Run schedule quantities determine the dates and quantities. Run schedule quantities are planned orders of the type PE that do not have to be released and that you do not have to convert into production or process orders to be able to carry out production. The requirements are generated by demand management, for example. Sales order quantities are delivered from stock and consume the planned independent requirement quantities in demand management, according to the planning strategy you select. A product cost collector is used to collect actual data and to settle costs.

289. Explain "Make-to-order production" in a nutshell in SAP S/4HANA?

The system creates one or several planned orders which directly reference the sales order item. The material is then manufactured on the basis of these planned orders. That is, production is triggered by the receipt of the sales orders. For component materials that are relevant to repetitive manufacturing, you use the product cost collector of the component to collect costs. On finished item level, you either use valuated or non-valuated material: Costs are collected by the sales order if you use non-valuated material and by the product cost collector if the material is valuated.

290. Explain "Staging materials using the pull list" in a nutshell in SAP S/4HANA?

You can use the pull list to control the in-house flow of material for supplying production with materials. A prerequisite for this is that the components required for production are already available (either produced in-house or procured externally) and must only be brought from their current storage location to the production storage location.

The pull list checks the stock situation at the production storage location and calculates the quantities of missing parts. You can create replenishment elements for these missing parts. You can stage the components by direct stock transfer or stock transfer reservation. You can also trigger replenishment by setting a Kanban to empty or by creating transfer requirements in Warehouse Management.

291. Explain "Monitoring with the Kanban board" in a nutshell?

You can use the Kanban board to monitor production progress. Irrespective of whether you are the supply source or the demand source, the Kanban board provides you with a detailed overview of the Kanban's in circulation. You can also use the Kanban board to change the status of the Kanban's. The following additional information is available, for example:

- You can display the control cycle, material, plant, actual quantity, status, date of the last status change and so on by double-clicking the individual Kanban's.

- You can display the control cycle data by double-clicking the appropriate row on the Kanban board.

- You can navigate to the stock/requirements list, the stock overview, or the material master for a control cycle.

- You can trigger the Kanban correction facility for a control cycle.

292. Explain "Cost accounting for Kanban" in a nutshell?

You have various options for controlling cost accounting for Kanban with in-house production depending on which replenishment elements are used. If you use:

- Run schedule quantities: The costs are collected in a product cost collector and can be settled periodically in product costing.
- Manual Kanban: The costs are also collected in a product cost collector.
- Production orders or process orders: The costs are either collected in a product cost collector if you want to analyze the costs by periods rather than by lot, or they are settled to the individual production orders/process orders.

Updates to the actual costs at the product cost collector can be triggered by logistical transactions (such as goods issues or confirmations) for production/process orders and run schedule headers. For example, goods issues for a production order or reporting point back flushes in repetitive manufacturing debit the product cost collector with actual costs. Goods receipts credit the product cost collector. Alternatively, the actual costs at the product cost collector can be updated directly through G/L account postings in Financial Accounting (FI), for example.

You can access reports and view the actual costs for the product cost collector. During the period-end closing, you can:

- Charge the product cost collector by means of template allocation.
- Reevaluate the activities at actual prices.
- Calculate overhead for the product cost collector.
- Calculate the value of your unfinished products (work in process) for the period.
- Calculate the variances of the period.
- Settle the work-in-process & variance(s) to other application components.

293. Explain "JIT Outbound Processing" in a nutshell?

Just in Time (JIT) Outbound Processing enables you to replenish direct materials required for manufacturing in the exact quantity and at exactly the time required. You can determine that the required materials are provided internally from a different location, for example. Or, you can specify that the required materials are provided by an external supplier. If you opt for material provision from an external supplier, you can use scheduling agreements with delivery schedules for procurement and production planning processes. JIT calls are used as a replenishment request and the fulfillment is done with reference to them.

294. Explain "Supply-to-production planning" in a nutshell?

You can use this feature for planning, triggering, and monitoring replenishment using summarized JIT calls. For each control cycle used for supply-to-production planning, the system calculates replenishment requirements taking account of:

● Open JIT calls

● Available stock at the production location

● A defined minimum stock level

● Component requirements from production planning.

295. Explain "Forwarded sequenced JIT call processing" in a nutshell?

You can use this feature to forward a group of components of an inbound sequenced JIT call received from your customer to an external supplier who will assemble and deliver the component group. You use control cycles to enable and define the replenishment process. You can send a delivery confirmation to your supplier which is used for the invoicing process.

296. Explain "Sample management" in a nutshell?

You use this feature for processing and managing samples.

Sample management allows you to:

● Flexibly plan the drawing of samples

● Identify samples

● Record inspection results for samples

● Manage the sample data.

297. Explain "Calibration inspections" in a nutshell in SAP S/4HANA?

Users may plan and perform calibration inspections of test equipment. Based on the inspection results, you can verify the accuracy and suitability of test equipment for an inspection.

298. Explain "Stability studies" in a nutshell in SAP S/4HANA?

You use this feature to track and examine how different environmental conditions (for example, temperature, brightness, moisture) affect a compound, a material, or a batch over a specified period of time.

299. Explain "Quality analytics" in a nutshell in SAP S/4HANA?

An integrated set of quality data allows you to quickly identify systematic errors, analyze problems, eliminate root causes, and respond faster to unforeseen events and deviations.

You can perform quality evaluations based on inspection results or based on issue data.

300. Explain "Audit management" in a nutshell in SAP S/4HANA?

An audit is a systematic examination for determining, evaluating, and documenting the extent to which an object fulfills predefined criteria. Audit management supports you in all phases of auditing.

301. Explain "Inventory management" in a nutshell in SAP S/4HANA?

The MRO extension of inventory management is capable of procuring and then stocking a part using its original manufacturer's part number in the parts planning and consumption.

The parts interchangeability feature allows the stocking of different manufacturers' parts that meet Form-Fit-Function rules, allowing MRP to calculate part demand and view stock across manufacturers' part numbers for part availability.

It also has the capability to stock and repair customer-owned parts that are segregated by customer numbers.

302. Explain "Maintenance Planning" in a nutshell in SAP S/4HANA?

This includes:

- Spare Parts Stock Calculation: This application determines an initial stock level for the part type required to supply a serviceable part, with probability of a specific percentage if the part in question fails. The probability is represented by the service level.

- Work Packaging and Sequencing (WPS): This application summarizes processes and activities for planning and performing large maintenance tasks.

- Mass Maintenance of Maintenance Plans: This function allows you to change several maintenance plans in the same way at the same time.

- Maintenance Program Definition: This component provides a workbench that you can use to transform complex maintenance requirements into maintenance plans within the maintenance execution system.

- Maintenance and Service Planning (MSP): You use MSP to carry out the following:

  o Strategic planning over a long-term horizon, such as 5-10 years, allowing you to determine the resources necessary to meet future maintenance demands

  o Tactical planning over a mid-term horizon, such as 1-18 months, to ensure that your maintenance objects remain serviceable, optimize utilization of your maintenance objects, and balance the resource load in your service areas.

303. Explain "Maintenance and Service Processing (MSP)" in a nutshell in SAP S/4HANA?

In maintenance and service processing, the primary objective is to ensure the hardware availability of technical objects. The process includes activities for tracking individual components during their entire life cycle, whether installed in the hardware, stored in a warehouse, or serviced in a workshop.

Components are exchanged if they cannot be repaired in time, have reached their life limits, or are listed in service bulletin directives for replacement. In the case of tables, an unserviceable component is placed in a warehouse and replaced by a new or serviceable component. In urgent cases (for example, if a component cannot be transferred to a line station in time), a component is taken from other equipment that is currently not in operation. Sometimes it is possible to swap identical components within an equipment number, instead of repairing the defective component.

MSP features include:

- Component Maintenance Cockpit (CMC)
- Subcontracting for MRO Processes
- Plant Maintenance and Customer Services (PM/CS) Orders in the MRO Process
- Assignment of PM/CS Orders to Projects
- Sharing of Spare Parts
- Configuration Control
- Logbook
- Integration of Service Processing with Warranty Claims.

304. Explain "Creating Maintenance Bills of Materials (BOMs)" in a nutshell in SAP S/4HANA?

A maintenance bill of material (BOM) is a complete, formally structured list of the components making up a technical object or an assembly. Maintenance BOMs support you when locating malfunctions by providing you with an overview of all components that make up a technical object. From this overview you can easily select the object for which you want to create a malfunction report. Furthermore, maintenance BOMs provide you with an overview of all spare parts used for the maintenance of a specific technical object, so they make spares planning considerably easier.

A maintenance BOM contains the object numbers of the individual components together with their quantity and unit of measure, and can be assigned to the master record of a technical object or material.

305. Explain benefits of "Maintenance Planning and Scheduling Business" in a nutshell in SAP S/4HANA?

Maintenance Planning and Scheduling helps you optimize the scope of work and effort required for inspection, maintenance, and planned repairs. Based on legal requirements, manufacturer recommendations, and cost analyses, you determine which preventive maintenance tasks are required, which work centers are needed, and how frequently preventive maintenance tasks have to be processed to avoid breakdown time. Maintenance plans support you in specifying maintenance cycles, scheduling maintenance calls, and determining the expected costs for a specific time period. In maintenance task lists you can describe a sequence of individual maintenance activities which must be performed repeatedly within your company. In addition, you can use 2D and 3D model views to visualize technical objects, spare parts, and instructions as well as to find the spare parts you need for carrying out maintenance tasks quicker and easier.

306. Explain benefits of "Maintenance Execution" in a nutshell in SAP S/4HANA?

Maintenance Execution allows you to perform planned and unplanned maintenance tasks. Maintenance planners can carry out preliminary costing, work scheduling, material provisioning, and resource planning. They provide maintenance workers with job lists so that they have easy access to all maintenance-related information. This leads to increased efficiency and productivity. Maintenance workers can review the jobs assigned to them and carry out the required maintenance work based on the tasks and operations in the order. While confirming that they have finished the job, they can enter measurement readings, which the system records in measurement documents.

307. Explain benefits of "Project Financial Control" in a nutshell in SAP S/4HANA?

This capability enables you to define work breakdown structures as a basis for hierarchical project accounting. You can plan costs and budgets and track actual costs that are tightly integrated with core business processes. This provides you with better insight into the project progress and your project financial performance and enables you to avoid cost overruns in time.

308. Explain use of "Project Versions" in a nutshell in SAP S/4HANA?

A project version shows the state of the project at a certain point in time or at a certain status. You can create as many project versions as required. Some features include:

- Document (as a history) the state of the project in the past
- Can be used for comparison purposes.

309. Explain benefits of "Project Logistics Control" in a nutshell in SAP S/4HANA?

This capability enables you define project structures consisting of work breakdown structures and network structure, plan and schedule project activities, control all procurement processes integrated with the core business process, and provide an insight into all logistic related execution aspects of a project.

For features related to work breakdown structures, refer to Project Financial Control.

310. Explain use of "Maintaining standard networks" in a nutshell in SAP S/4HANA?

- You use this feature to maintain the standard network structures for your project. When creating any standard operative networks or networks the project-neutral network structure can be used as a template.

- While creating project templates you may link standard networks with standard work breakdown structures.

311. Explain use of "Maintaining operative networks" in a nutshell in SAP S/4HANA?

- You can copy from a standard network or an operative network to create a new operative network. If you have assigned a standard network to a standard WBS, you can create an operative WBS at the same time that you create an operative network.

- You can create milestones in networks, standard networks, work breakdown structures (WBS) and standard work breakdown structures (standard WBS).

312. Explain use of "Network Scheduling" in a nutshell in SAP S/4HANA?

Scheduling determines the earliest and latest start and finish dates for carrying out activities in the network and calculates the required capacity requirements. A network is always scheduled forwards and backwards.

- Forward scheduling calculates the earliest start and finish dates of activities (earliest dates) and the scheduled finish date of the network.

- Backward scheduling calculates the latest start and finish dates of activities (latest dates) and the scheduled start date of the network.

In a complex project, the dependencies in a project can make the activities in one network dependent on the completion of activities in another network. You can use the function for the overall network scheduling where the networks are linked through certain relationships.

313. Explain use of "Bill of Materials" in a nutshell in SAP S/4HANA?

A formally structured list of the components that make up a product is abbreviated as "A bill of material (BOM)". The list contains the object number of each component, together with the quantity and unit of measure. The components are known as BOM items. They contain important basic data for numerous areas of a company.

314. Explain use of "Product structures" in a nutshell in SAP S/4HANA?

A product structure is an enhanced engineering bill of material (BOM). It consists of a set of hierarchically ordered objects with the purpose of documenting one product or a set of similar products. This is effective for high-volume, repetitive manufacturing, for example, in the automotive industry, as well as for complex machinery and equipment.

If you work with products that have many variants and a large number of components, you can use product structure management to optimize process support from early engineering, to hand-over to manufacturing.

Product visualization tools allow you to manage geometric data and view digital mockups in your product structures via viewable files.

315. Explain benefits of "Product structures" in a nutshell in SAP S/4HANA?

Product structures provide the following benefits:

- Possible to create and maintain a product structure without assigning materials
- A redundancy-free description of products or product families with many variants
- Variant configuration and variant management capabilities
- The option of working with both configurable and configured materials
- Continuous modeling from an early stage to the manufacturing handover
- Modeling of functional structures (with no requirement for material number references)

- Template structures for the creation of product structures and the standardization of product descriptions
- A consistent data basis for different views of the product and for all enterprise areas.

316. Explain use of "Managing geometric data" in a nutshell in SAP S/4HANA?

You can assign geometric data to support the transition of transformation matrices into product structures. Together with viewable files, the geometric data enables dynamic viewing based on simulations offered by the product structure.

317. Explain use of "Modeling product structures" in a nutshell in SAP S/4HANA?

You can use product structures to model a multilevel product hierarchy. When modeling your product structure, you have the flexibility to develop the structure and the variants without having to create master data. You can model a configurable product with multiple combinations and possible scenarios.

318. Explain use of "Simulating the product configuration" in a nutshell in SAP S/4HANA?

You can check the product configuration by simulating the explosion of a product structure for a specific set of configuration parameters. You can save, edit, and activate these simulations.

319. Explain use of "Viewing digital mockups" in a nutshell in SAP S/4HANA?

Digital mockups, which are triggered at various stages of new product design, enable design engineers, product engineers, and manufacturing engineers to study the content developed before it is handed over to the next department. You can view a digital mockup in the product structure.

320. Explain use of "Embedded Software Management" in a nutshell in SAP S/4HANA?

Embedded software is computer software that is embedded in one or multiple products. It provides functions together with various hardware and systems. For example, embedded software can be used to control or optimize the functions of the mechanical part or the electrical part of a product.

If you work with products that have one or multiple pieces of embedded software, you can use embedded software management to view and manage your software.

321. Explain use of "Engineering Change Management" in a nutshell in SAP S/4HANA?

Engineering change management can be used to manage various aspects of engineering basic data (for example, bills of materials, materials, and documents) with structured change process. The engineering change management is a crucial component to ensure effective change handling in product development.

322. Explain use of "Engineering cockpit" in a nutshell in SAP S/4HANA?

You use this feature to get an overview of engineering changes and engineering progress for different business objects.

323. Explain use of "Recipe and Formula Development" in a nutshell in SAP S/4HANA?

You use Recipe Development to describe the manufacturing of products or the execution of a process. Recipes comprise information about the products and components of a process, the process steps to be executed, and the resources required for the production.

The recipe types in Recipe Development enable you to create a general description of the requirements or concrete procedural instructions depending on your needs. Making the data of enterprise-wide recipes more concrete allows you derive site- and plant-specific recipes from it.

324. Explain use of "Access Control Management" in a nutshell in SAP S/4HANA?

Access Control Management allows you to control access to specifications, recipes and documents. You can grant access to users or user groups using access control contexts.

325. Explain use of "Handing Over Product Structure for Production" in a nutshell in SAP S/4HANA?

You can use this business process to define a transition of product structures from engineering, such as bills of material or product structures to manufacturing. During the handover, a new manufacturing product structure is created from scratch or an already synchronized manufacturing structure is updated based on changes from the engineering product structure.

The process is focused to keep the engineering and manufacturing product structure synchronous, while only the manufacturing product structure is updated.

Changes from engineering can be handed over to the manufacturing product structure with or without change management.

326. Explain use of "Product Marketability and Chemical Compliance" in a nutshell in SAP S/4HANA?

With the product marketability and chemical compliance solution you manage chemical compliance for your products across your organization. The features of this business solution support you to ensure product marketability and brand protection, and to reduce compliance costs. They enable you to manage regulatory requirements and compliance assessments of your product portfolio.

327. Explain use of "Dangerous Goods Management" in a nutshell in SAP S/4HANA?

This process enables you to manage data which is needed to classify and process dangerous goods in the logistics chain according to dangerous goods regulations. Compliance with regulations of dangerous goods is an important component of product stewardship to ensure safe packaging and transportation of dangerous goods.

328. Explain use of "Safety Data Sheet Management and Hazard Label Data" in a nutshell in SAP S/4HANA?

With this business solution you manage and create safety data sheets (SDS) and labels according to chemical regulations and requirements. An SDS is an important component of product stewardship. It is legally required in most countries and regions of the world to ensure safe handling of chemicals and other hazardous products. SDS formats can vary from source to source depending on national requirements. SDSs are a widely-used system for cataloging information on chemicals, chemical compounds, and chemical mixtures. SDS information may include instructions for the safe use and potential hazards associated with a particular material or product. The SDS should be available for reference in the area where the chemicals are being stored or in use.

Label and safety data sheets are important sources of information on hazards, instructions and information on the safe storage, handling, use, and disposal of hazardous substances. This information helps you to minimize risks when using hazardous substances.

329. Explain use of "Commodity Sales" in a nutshell in SAP S/4HANA?

With Commodity Sales you enter, process and manage your sales documents, deliveries and billing documents for commodities of all industries, perform a simple to use formula-based commodity pricing, also for future dates, use the market data management based on derivative contract specifications, enter and allocate price fixations, and perform period-end valuations.

330. Explain use of "Period-End Valuation" in a nutshell in SAP S/4HANA?

For deliveries of commodities with goods issues, where the commodity price is floating (for example, due to market price changes), and a final invoice was not posted yet on or before the valuation key date, the period-end valuation is used to calculate the accrual amount from the difference between an anticipated fi-nal invoice amount and the posted amount.

For the period-end valuation, Commodity Sales provides several transactions such as to create and post accrual documents, to generate worklists, to verify valuation results, and to perform completeness checks.

331. Explain use of "Commodity Position Reporting" in a nutshell in SAP S/4HANA?

Commodity Position Reporting enables you to analyze the price risk quantities of commodity positions resulting from logistics transactions and material stock.

332. Explain use of "Mark-to-Market Reporting" in a nutshell in SAP S/4HANA?

The Mark-to-Market Reporting calculates and shows you the undiscounted MtM values for unrealized logistics documents and material stock, as well as the MtM changes between two points of time.

333. Explain use of "Profit and Loss Reporting" in a nutshell in SAP S/4HANA?

The Profit and Loss Reporting enhances the Mark-to-Market Reporting and is aimed to explain the root causes for changes in MtM values within a set period. MtM values can vary due to, for example, changes of market quotations, FX rates, as well as modified pricing data and/or commodity quantities in logistics documents and of material stock. The P/L attribution shows how much each event and market price movement has attributed to the MtM delta values for a certain period.

334. Explain use of "Subscription Billing and Revenue Management" in a nutshell in SAP S/4HANA?

Subscription Billing and Revenue Management monetizes digital business models. It is tailored towards the requirements of corporates across all industries and lines of business with high volumes of customers, subscriptions, and pay-per-use transactions. It provides flexible billing processes, enables multi-sided business models, and manages resulting revenues and expenses with high automation and throughput. Key business and process capabilities include the following:

- Subscription business models with recurring- and one-time charges
- Rating and billing of millions of usage transactions converged from multiple transactional platforms
- Complex, volume-based discounts and surcharges
- Revenue sharing and partner settlement.

335. Explain use of "Convergent Invoicing" in a nutshell in SAP S/4HANA?

Convergent Invoicing merges information from several billing streams as well as individually rated events. It enables service providers to consolidate charges into a single invoice and give a complete view of the customer. Providers can accommodate partnerships with third parties and ramp up new services by clearly delineating which party is responsible for any given charge. They can also manage sophisticated rules for invoice-level discounting. By greatly simplifying complex billing processes, providers can give customers a single, consolidated invoice, while delivering better, more personalized services.

336. Explain use of "Receivables Management and Payment" in a nutshell in SAP S/4HANA?

Receivables Management and Payment Handling receives and manages a large number of postings, for example created by billing processes, and uploads these postings to the general ledger.

All commonly used payment methods for incoming and outgoing payments in your enterprise are processed.

Receivables Management and Payment Handling enables billing professionals to assign individual clearing strategies, automate payment reconciliation, and generate reports aligned with accounting principles. Processing payments in a highly automated environment enables the billing team to reduce days' sales outstanding and processing costs.

The software has been tailored towards the requirements of corporates across all industries and lines of business with high volumes of customers, subscriptions, and pay-per-use transactions. The processes provided with Receivables Management and Payment Handling are highly flexible to allow for a maximum of automation as well as mechanisms to ensure outstanding system performance and scalability.

337. Explain use of "Credit and Collections Management" in a nutshell in SAP S/4HANA?

Credit and Collections Management provides reliable, comprehensive credit scoring of new and existing customers based on historical customer data integrated with external credit rating agencies. It fully automates routine tasks in the collections process for mass volumes of customers, such as the calculation of interest payments. Billing personnel can change and continuously optimize collections strategies by using Champion/Challenger analysis as well as in-house teams and external collections agencies. A complete picture of the credit and collection history of new and existing customers enables providers to reduce days sales outstanding and the risk of nonpayment, while retaining loyal customers.

338. Explain use of "Integration of SAP S/4HANA with Machine Learning Intelligence" in a nutshell?

SAP S/4HANA supports the integration with a machine learning system (currently SAP S/4HANA Cloud, intelligent insights for procurement) to allow users to optimize their procurement processes.

Key Features

If a machine learning system (for example, SAP S/4HANA Cloud, intelligent insights for procurement) is integrated and supports the features listed below, SAP S/4HANA enables you to use the following key features:

Key Feature	Use
Proposal for creation of catalog items	You can identify free-text purchase requisition items with similar descriptions. The system uses this information to propose the creation of new catalog items. Purchasers can negotiate lower prices for highly requested items identified by the system.
Proposal of material groups	When users create a free-text purchase requisition, the system classifies the description and suggests the most probable material groups.
Proposals for materials without contracts	The system compares materials without a contract to materials with a contract and then proposes the creation of a request for quotation for specific materials. Based on the request for quotation, a new contract can be created.

339. Explain use of "Central Procurement" in a nutshell in SAP S/4HANA?

With Central Procurement, you can integrate your SAP S/4HANA system with some other enterprise resource planning systems in your system landscape (that is, SAP S/4HANA, SAP S/4HANA Cloud, or SAP ERP) to offer centralized procurement processes over your entire system landscape. SAP S/4HANA acts as a hub system and the enterprise resource planning systems act as connected systems in this integration scenario.

340. Explain use of "Central Requisitioning" in a nutshell in SAP S/4HANA?

The Central Requisitioning scenario facilitates employees to have a unified shopping experience where they can create self-service requisitions in an SAP S/4HANA system (which acts as a hub system). You can create items for materials or services extracted from external catalogs and from an integrated cross-content search based on SAP S/4HANA. Additionally, you can create free-text items if none of the materials in the connected system or the ones extracted into the hub system matches your requirements. This scenario also enables you to confirm the ordered goods or services in the hub system.

341. Explain use of "Central Purchase Contracts" in a nutshell in SAP S/4HANA?

In an integrated procurement scenario, you can create central purchase contracts. These are global, long-term agreements between organizations and suppliers regarding the supply of materials or the performance of services within a certain period as per predefined terms and conditions. Central purchase contracts enable purchasers from various parts of a company in different locations to take advantage of the negotiated terms and conditions. Central purchase contracts are created in the SAP S/4HANA system (which acts as a hub system) and distributed to the connected systems, such as SAP ERP, SAP S/4HANA Cloud, or SAP S/4HANA.

342. Explain use of "Central Purchasing" in a nutshell in SAP S/4HANA?

The Central Purchasing scenario provides a single point of access to display and manage purchasing documents centrally. The purchasing documents include purchase requisitions and purchase orders. These documents can be the ones that are created in the SAP S/4HANA system (which acts as a hub system) or the ones that have been extracted from the connected systems. SAP S/4HANA, SAP S/4HANA Cloud, or SAP ERP act as connected systems. Central Purchasing provides the flexibility of connecting multiple systems across an organization and carrying out procurement processes centrally.

343. Explain use of "Central Purchasing Analytics" in a nutshell in SAP S/4HANA?

Central Purchasing Analytics provides users with centralized analyses and the necessary capabilities to better understand the procurement areas – both on a holistic level and on a more fine-granular level relating to connected systems. Strategic buyers can analyze the consumption of central contracts across entire organizations, as well as identify where global contracts are not being properly utilized. Additionally, monitoring the global purchasing spend using drill-down capabilities pinpoints the spend volume across the entire organization.

344. Explain use of "Commodity Procurement" in a nutshell in SAP S/4HANA?

With Commodity Procurement you enter, process and manage your purchasing contracts, purchase orders, goods receipts and invoices for commodities of all industries, perform a simple to use formula-based commodity pricing, also for future dates, use the market data management based on derivative contract specifications, enter and allocate price fixations, and perform period-end valuations.

345. Explain use of "Invoice Collaboration (SAP Fieldglass)" in a nutshell in SAP S/4HANA?

SAP Fieldglass provides a cloud-based solution for managing contingent workforce and service procurement. SAP S/4HANA currently supports an integration scenario for invoice handling with SAP Fieldglass that is enabled by the exchange of messages.

346. Explain use of "Extended Warehouse Management" in a nutshell in SAP S/4HANA?

Extended warehouse management provides tools for managing and processing material movements flexibly, to optimize more complex warehouse processes.

347. Explain use of "Yard Management" in a nutshell in SAP S/4HANA?

The yard is where you maintain vehicles and transportation units that arrive or depart from your warehouse.

You can use yard management to move transportation units from one yard bin to another inside a yard. Possible types of yard movement are as follows:

- The transportation unit arrives at the checkpoint and is moved to a parking space or to the door.
- You move a transportation unit from a parking space to the door, or from the door to a parking space.
- You move a transportation unit in the yard from one parking space to another, or from one door to another.

348. Explain use of "Labor Management" in a nutshell in SAP S/4HANA?

You can plan labor times and resources in your warehouse, by classifying, measuring, planning, and simulating the activities in your warehouse.

You can compare and evaluate the performance of your warehouse employees based on engineered labor standards. You evaluate performance on an individual level or based on teams or shifts.

After the work has been performed, you can compare the planned and actual times, and trigger incentives such as bonus payments using the HR system.

You can use short-term operational planning match the workload with the number of employees in the warehouse.

You can import or maintain time and attendance data in extended warehouse management.

349. Explain use of "Cross-Docking" in a nutshell in SAP S/4HANA?

You can create and confirm tasks to transport products or handling units from goods receipt to goods issue without put away occurring in between. Using cross-docking enables you to fulfil urgent sales orders, or to reduce processing and storage costs.

You can perform cross-docking in the following ways:

- Opportunistic cross-docking

  Extended warehouse management can determine the cross-docking relevance of the products after they have physically arrived in the warehouse

- Merchandise distribution

Extended warehouse management receives inbound and outbound delivery documents from the system which contain the merchandise distribution process methods and the purchase order item. For the inbound delivery, extended warehouse management first considers all outbound deliveries that have the same reference number. In addition, extended warehouse management uses the merchandise distribution process to determine the warehouse process type, and to perform the merchandise distribution cross-docking according to Customizing.

350. Explain use of "Warehouse Billing" in a nutshell in SAP S/4HANA?

Warehouse billing allows you to perform the following activities with a connected SAP Transportation Management (SAP TM) system:

- Record the quantity of warehouse services used for services agreed upon in an agreement in the connected SAP TM system.

- Send this quantity information back to the connected SAP TM system for charge calculation and settlement based on the charges you have agreed to in the agreement.

    Warehouse billing allows you to perform the following activities with an embedded Transportation Management (TM):

- Record and send quantity information to embedded TM for self-billing or charge calculation and settlement purposes.

351. Explain use of "Advanced Transportation Management" in a nutshell in SAP S/4HANA?

Advanced Transportation Management (TM) in SAP S/4HANA supports the entire transportation chain. You can manage the transportation demands by planning, optimizing, tendering, subcontracting, and settlement of freight processes. Also, you can book carriers in accordance with the requirements of international trade and hazardous goods.

TM supports the following end-to-end processes:

- Domestic and international transportation

- Inbound and outbound freight management based on sales orders, purchase orders, deliveries, stock transfers, and returns

- Embedded analytics and key performance indicators for real-time performance visibility.

352. Explain use of "Strategic freight management" in a nutshell in SAP S/4HANA?

To support your freight agreement negotiations, you can use strategic freight procurement. It helps you to negotiate rates with carriers to transport cargo between specific locations (trade lanes) and agree on a contract (agreement) with the carriers. TM provides the tools that you need to request rate quotations, evaluate responses, and award the transportation business to carriers.

353. Explain use of "Forwarding order management" in a nutshell in SAP S/4HANA?

You can use forwarding order management to create, edit, and confirm forwarding orders from your ordering parties. You can also already specify the route and have the transportation charges calculated here. The orders then form the basis for transportation planning.

In addition to creating the forwarding order, you can also enter the data as a forwarding quotation and send it to the ordering party. You can then create a forwarding order based on the forwarding quotation.

354. Explain use of "Freight order management" in a nutshell in SAP S/4HANA?

In freight order management, you can create and edit freight orders and freight bookings. These documents contain information required for transportation planning and execution, such as source and destination locations, dates or times, product information, and resources used. You can create freight orders directly or in transportation planning. For example, you can assign freight units to the freight orders and have the system calculate the transportation charges. You can perform carrier selection, assign the freight orders directly to a carrier as a suborder, or perform tendering.

355. Explain use of "Tendering" in a nutshell in SAP S/4HANA?

You can use this process to send out freight requests for quotation (freight RFQs) to one or more carriers according to a tendering plan. You can use a freight RFQ tendering process to send out one or more freight RFQs. You can send the freight RFQs manually, or enable the system to send them out automatically. You can also use a direct tendering process to send a road freight order (road FO) directly to a specified carrier without creating a freight RFQ. Carriers can confirm or reject the road FOs. Unlike the freight RFQ process, the system generally awards a carrier if he or she does not reject the road FO within a given time limit.

Direct tendering can be created and started manually by the user or automatically by the system. Furthermore, you can use freight bookings to book freight space in advance, for example, with a shipping company. You can then perform the execution on these documents.

356. Explain use of "Advanced Available to Promise" in a nutshell in SAP S/4HANA?

Internal sales representatives, order fulfillment managers and order fulfillment specialists require mechanisms to configure, execute and monitor availability checks and optimize the distribution of supply. This is particularly important when the availability of materials needed to confirm requirements is limited. You can use the advanced available-to-promise (aATP) capabilities to confirm on which date and in which quantity a requirement can be fulfilled.

357. Explain use of "Product Availability Check" in a nutshell in SAP S/4HANA?

You can use this feature to determine on which date and in which quantity a requirement can be confirmed, based on a specified checking rule and the current supply situation for a specific material. The availability check takes concurrent requirements of differing types and their respective confirmation situation into consideration.

358. Explain use of "Product Allocation" in a nutshell in SAP S/4HANA?

You can use this feature to allocate material quantities for a specific time period and to characteristic values combination for sales orders and stock transport orders, against which availability checks can be run.

You can monitor the product allocation situation for product allocation objects, allocation periods, characteristic value combinations and order items during a specific time period. Using the displayed data, you can take action to optimize the overall product allocation situation.

359. Explain use of "Backorder Processing" in a nutshell in SAP S/4HANA?

You can use this feature to re-prioritize sales orders and stock transport orders and perform automated mass availability checks to ensure that a limited supply of material is distributed in accordance with a specific strategy. Optionally, your system assigns specific supply elements to the individual requirements.

You can monitor the check results and, if necessary, re-run the check to improve the confirmations for the requirements.

360. Explain use of "Geographical Enablement Framework" in a nutshell in SAP S/4HANA?

Map-driven user experiences are ubiquitous, and they are enabled through mobile devices with built-in GPS receivers. Whereas consumers are quite satisfied by easily locating places and checking for directions, requirements in asset intensive industries such as Utilities, Oil & Gas, Mining, Public Services, and Transportation/ Rail go far beyond simple use cases. Existing GIS (geographic information system) solutions that maintain multiple layers of map information, visualization of linear assets, and objects represented by polygons (example: a certain area of land) need to be merged with their related business processes and reflected in SAP solutions.

361. Explain key features of "SAP Geographical Enablement Framework" in a nutshell in SAP S/4HANA?

For extending business data with spatial attributes for SAP S/4HANA functions the SAP Geographical Enablement framework works as the foundation. It helps companies to develop geo-spatially enriched business data and makes them accessible from within SAP S/4HANA functions, as well as external GIS systems. It is being delivered with a standalone Geometry-Explorer, Geometry-Editor, and a template for the Business Partner business object as an example for spatially enabling other business objects. Please note that you might need a separate license.

Key Feature	Use
Geometry Explorer	The framework provides a standalone web-based Geometry Explorer. It allows the end user to view both business data from SAP S/4HANA functions and engineering data from GIS systems on the same map to obtain better insights. It also allows the end user to access multiple SAP S/4HANA functions directly from the map to improve efficiency.
Geometry Editor	The framework provides a standalone web-based Geometry Editor. It allows the end user to search, view, and update geometries for any geo-enabled SAP business object.

Key Feature	Use
External Connectivity	Framework exposes the geometries and attributes of geo-enabled SAP business objects as feature classes, to be consumed using standard GIS tools.
Framework Development Technology	The framework provides APIs for application development; it also provides geometry-buffering functionality for synchronization with the embedded map user interface, while updating geometry and application data concurrently.

362. Explain use of "Legal Content Overview" in a nutshell in SAP S/4HANA?

Legal Content Overview analyzes the most important legal transactions, contexts, and documents that you need to process. The graphical representation of the most critical tasks summarizes key information from the underlying apps that you are working on, so that you can analyze and identify upcoming important dates, reminders, and transactions and take quicker decisions. There are various actionable cards showing vital information ranked as per their expiration, risk or health.

363. Explain use of "Managing Categories" in a nutshell in SAP S/4HANA?

Categories classify business objects such as contexts and legal transactions. You can use categories to classify legal content. Legal content is created by or exchanged between legal departments. Based on the categories that are assigned to the legal content business objects, the legal content can be classified.

364. Explain use of "Managing Legal Transactions" in a nutshell in SAP S/4HANA?

Legal transactions are created based on a legal content request and is used to manage the legal content through its lifecycle. For this, the legal transaction collects all the information and material that is connected with the legal content: the parties involved in the creation of the legal content internally as well as externally, the deadlines that need to be observed, the tasks that need to be completed, and the documents that need to be generated in the process or are linked to the legal transaction.

365. Explain use of "Agricultural Contract Management" in a nutshell in SAP S/4HANA?

SAP S/4HANA Industry solution for Agricultural Contract Management (ACM) provides a single source of truth for handling a diverse range of commodities contracts throughout their life-cycles. It supports a comprehensive range of business scenarios, agricultural-specific terms and conditions, market-based pricing and processes to effectively integrate finance and inventory.

366. Explain use of "Contract Tolerances" in a nutshell in SAP S/4HANA?

You can use this feature to define tolerances for overfill or underfill quantity that is calculated by comparing the actual delivered quantity to the planned contracted quantity. Defining the contract tolerances provides the ability to price over the delivered quantity separately.

367. Explain use of "Quality Characteristic-based Discounts and Premiums" in a nutshell in SAP S/4HANA?

You can use this feature to leverage the load-based captured qualities, such as moisture, to calculate:

- Quantity adjustments, such as shrinkage due to high moisture content

- Discounts and premiums for settlements.

368. Explain use of "Flexible Contract Assignment Framework" in a nutshell in SAP S/4HANA?

You can use this feature to flexibly assign and reassign the loads (deliveries) to the contracts without the need for cancelling and rebooking the documents, in case of goods movements, for example.

369. Explain use of "Flexible Pricing" in a nutshell in SAP S/4HANA?

You can use this feature to flexibly price and reprice the contracts based on the Commodity Pricing Engine (CPE). A price can be assigned to the specific market exchange and future periods.

The following pricing actions are supported:

- Set a price
- Lift a price
- Roll a price

Setting, lifting and rolling a price in a contract via Commodity Derivative Order Trade Execution (CDOTE) is supported.

370. Explain use of "Load Data Capture" in a nutshell in SAP S/4HANA?

The Load Data Capture is a tool that gives the end user a unique interface to capture all required information (weight, quality, vehicle and so on) for incoming and outgoing loads. The required documents, such as deliveries and goods movements, are processed by the transaction in the background without the need for an additional user interaction.

371. Explain use of "Spot Purchase" in a nutshell in SAP S/4HANA?

You can use this feature to process the spot purchases in which goods receipts take place without the prior contracts or purchase orders. The background contract creation based on the receipt information is supported.

372. Explain use of "Provisional and Final Settlements" in a nutshell in SAP S/4HANA?

You can use this feature to define the contract terms that have to be fulfilled before a settlement is set to the final status. Prior to the fulfillment of the contract terms, the status is provisional.

For a provisional settlement, only a certain percentage of the overall amount can be considered. For example, 80% of the calculated amount is charged in the provisional settlement and the remaining delta will be charged at the time of the final settlement.

For provisional settlements, priced contracts are not required, while market prices can be used prior to the final setting of the contract prices.

373. Explain use of "Revenue Recognition Process" in a nutshell in SAP S/4HANA?

You can use this feature to defer the realization of the revenues unless certain requirements, such as title transfer and other contract terms, are fulfilled.

374. Explain use of "Intercompany End-to-End Process" in a nutshell in SAP S/4HANA?

You can use this feature to execute end-to-end intercompany processes from contract creation, goods movements, and contract reassignment to incremental settlement and revenue recognition.

The following title transfer scenarios are supported:

- Origin
- Destination
- In-Transit.

375. Explain use of "Intracompany End-to-End Process" in a nutshell in SAP S/4HANA?

You can use this feature to execute end-to-end intracompany processes from contract creation, goods movements to settlement.

The following title transfer scenarios are supported:

- Origin
- Destination
- In-Transit.

376. Explain use of "Commingled Stock" in a nutshell in SAP S/4HANA?

You can use this feature to manage the third party stocks at your locations as well as your own stocks at the third party locations by tracking all deliveries in and out of the commingled stocks with the detailed quality information. The deliveries into commingled stock can be assigned to storage agreements from which the associated information about warehouse receipt (negotiable or non-negotiable) can be captured.

This feature provides the capabilities, such as:

- Load out including load out matching
- Purchase from the commingled stock
- In-store purchase and sales
- Calculation of necessary storage quantity adjustments
- Split of an inbound commingled load between several counterparties at the time of load data capture and application.

377. Explain use of "Vendor Split" in a nutshell in SAP S/4HANA?

You can use this feature to split one load between multiple different vendors. For example, it is possible to split the load of one truck by assigning a partial quantity to the contract of one vendor, while assigning the remaining quantity to another contract owned by the different vendor.

378. Explain use of "Washouts" in a nutshell in SAP S/4HANA?

This feature allows two trading parties who have the same contract terms (such as commodity, quantity and delivery period) to agree to mutually offset and settle the contract without any movement of the goods.

379. Explain use of "Position Reporting - Price Type Report" in a nutshell in SAP S/4HANA?

The price type report is a period-based report which provides a holistic view over the contractually agreed quantities that are either fully priced, partially priced or unpriced.

380. Explain use of "Position Reporting - Premium Report" in a nutshell in SAP S/4HANA?

The premium position report is a period-based report which provides an overview of the basis risk without considering the futures risk.

381. Explain use of "Position Reporting - Slate Report" in a nutshell in SAP S/4HANA?

The slate report is a period-based report which provides an overview of future price fixation from the logistical contracts as well as from the future derivatives.

382. Explain use of "Mark-to-Market Report (for physical contracts)" in a nutshell in SAP S/4HANA?

The mark-to-market (MtM) report enables you to value the fixed contract prices against the latest market prices of a defined market exchange and a future period to calculate a gain or loss.

The MtM report is available in the following versions:

- Current
- End-of-Day
- Day-over-Day.

383. Explain use of "Stock Mark-to-Market Report" in a nutshell in SAP S/4HANA?

The stock mark-to-market (MtM) report provides the ability to value inventory against the latest market prices to calculate a gain or loss.

384. Explain use of "Profit and Loss Analysis" in a nutshell in SAP S/4HANA?

The profit and loss (PnL) analysis enables you to utilize several reports that attribute the overall profit and loss from physical trading operations to impacting factors that are related to the commodity trading business.

The following reports are provided:

- Beginning Position
- New Activity.

385. Explain use of "Settlement - Lien Management" in a nutshell in SAP S/4HANA?

The settlement lien process provides the ability to capture vendor-specific liens as a master data object. When creating a settlement group, the liens serve as a grouping split criteria to ensure that all units of a group have common liens.

386. Explain use of "Weighted Average Calculation for Physical Inventory" in a nutshell in SAP S/4HANA?

The weighted average calculation is a process which is automatically triggered for inbound processes via LDC, and calculates the weighted average quality factor of a given discount premium quality schedule (DPQS) characteristic. This feature also provides tools to monitor, and if needed, to correct the average calculated by the system.

387. Explain use of "Back-to-Back Process - Sales Division" in a nutshell in SAP S/4HANA?

The back-to-back process allows you to purchase goods from a vendor and directly sell them to a customer without a physical movement through an owned location. In this case, the physical movement is directly from the vendor to the customer. While in-transit the goods can also be diverted to a customer which is different from the customer originally planned.

388. Explain use of "Document Flow Work center" in a nutshell in SAP S/4HANA?

You can use this feature to view the entire document flow of an end-to-end process, supported by various selection criteria. It further enables to manually reverse either the application, settlement or Load Data Capture document including automatic reversal of all follow-on documents from the work center.

389. Explain use of "Fee Accrual" in a nutshell in SAP S/4HANA?

    This feature provides the ability to accrue the financial impact of pre-defined fees prior to invoicing or realization.

390. Explain use of "Contract Offers" in a nutshell in SAP S/4HANA?

    You can use this feature to create contract offers with a target strike price. The APIs for sharing information with external systems are delivered, which also help in converting offers into the contracts. A worklist is also being provided to help in converting offers into the contracts.

391. Explain use of "No Price Established Fees" in a nutshell in SAP S/4HANA?

    You can use the No Price Established (NPE) fees to calculate the duration how long a load was applied against an unpriced contract and charge accordingly for this period. The settlement of NPE fees provides the possibility to calculate an in-charge and a periodic re-occurring charge.

392. Explain use of "Freight Charges within Commodity Settlement" in a nutshell in SAP S/4HANA?

    You can use this feature to manually enter freight within an ACM settlement unit to capture the freight responsibility per counterparty. The feature supports the ability to capture the freight obligation from the load location to the incoterm location and the obligation from the incoterm location to the final destination. The corresponding freight charges are automatically added or deducted from the settlement net amount.

393. Explain use of "Quote Contracts" in a nutshell in SAP S/4HANA?

    You can use this feature to create non-position relevant and period restricted quote contracts in ACM. A worklist is provided to monitor open quotes, change statuses and create one or multiple contracts with your counterparty for each quote. The worklist provides the ability to monitor which contract has been created for quote. Quotes expire by time not by quantity.

394. Explain use of "Master Data Management" in a nutshell in SAP S/4HANA?

Master data is used to support operational processes in all areas of merchandise management or the fashion business. Master data contains the most important information about sites and business partners, such as suppliers and customers, as well as about all articles.

Master data management significantly reduces the time required to perform tasks because data is proposed automatically and is based on one single source of truth. Master data objects such as assortments or different kinds of product taxonomies facilitate the daily work of different retail or fashion specialists and help processes run smoothly.

395. Explain use of "Season management" in a nutshell in SAP S/4HANA?

- Use seasons for time-dependent structuring by bundling articles according to their limited product life cycle.

    Seasonal attributes are especially but not limited to fashion articles, for example, snow shovels are seasonal. Examples of seasons are summer, winter, and fall; however, a season can also be defined at a more detailed level, by collection or theme.

- Control logistical processes, such as sales and purchasing, based on the parameters maintained for different seasons.

396. Explain use of "Value-added-services management" in a nutshell in SAP S/4HANA?

Manage value-added services that enhance the value, worth, functionality, or usefulness of ordered articles.

Value-added services can be either articles or activities such as putting shirts on hangers, ironing, or labeling.

397. Explain use of "Global data synchronization" in a nutshell in SAP S/4HANA?

Procure, track, and update article master data from suppliers quickly and easily to optimize master data exchange.

398. Explain use of "Assortment Management" in a nutshell in SAP S/4HANA?

Companies strive to offer products in the right place and at the right time in order to meet consumer needs and expectations. To achieve this goal and support their retail processes, companies use assortments to model the assignments of the product mix (articles) to stores or store clusters according to aspects such as regional considerations.

399. Explain use of "Merchandise Buying" in a nutshell in SAP S/4HANA?

Retailers need to be able to source and buy merchandise and services using procurement processes and control mechanisms across the supply chain. Through effective buying processes, companies can procure goods faster and at lower cost from suppliers globally in order to:

- Contribute to the bottom line through informed negotiating, while achieving compliance and increasing automation.
- Reduce cost and react flexibly to dynamic market conditions.
- Support effective sourcing, contracts, operational buying, and management of large volumes of invoices.
- Adopt buying processes to specific merchandise and handle purchase orders efficiently and accurately.
- Increase procurement process efficiency and transparency through order consolidation.

400. Explain use of "Vendor-Managed Inventory" in a nutshell in SAP S/4HANA?

Close collaboration between business partners along the supply chain is of major importance with regard to streamlining logistical processes and ensuring that consumers are not faced with out-of-stock situations in stores.

In a vendor-managed-inventory business model, the task of ensuring that merchandise is available in stores is handled by the suppliers or manufacturers. To enable business partners to fulfil this task to the best of their ability, retailers need to provide the necessary information, including sales and inventory data.

401. Explain use of "Replenishment Planning" in a nutshell in SAP S/4HANA?

Companies often face the challenge of having to deliver optimum of amounts merchandise to a large number of stores on a regular basis. To achieve this, automated processes can be implemented to optimize and integrate merchandise flow across the supply chain, including processes that involve third parties. One of the methods is the pull principle: Demand originating from the recipients is bundled and procured. Replenishment is a pull process used to supply stores with merchandise on a demand-driven basis.

402. Explain use of "Demand Forecasting" in a nutshell in SAP S/4HANA?

Companies use planned demand data to support requirements planning methods in order to optimize stock levels across the supply chain and thereby better meet consumer needs and expectations.

403. Explain use of "Inventory Management" in a nutshell in SAP S/4HANA?

Companies need to manage inventory, that is, the quantities and the value information for articles carried at sites need to be managed across many locations and channels. Goods movements need to be reflected in inventory, such as an increase in inventory when a goods receipt is posted or a decrease in inventory when a goods issue for a sales transaction is posted. Physical inventory supports the processes of counting article quantities and posting the resulting adjustments. The transparency of inventory information is crucial to the success of any company with retail processes.

A sales order represents an agreement between a retailer and a customer concerning the sale and delivery of goods. Sales order fulfillment comprises the follow-on processes in the supply chain that result in the handover of merchandise to a customer and is completed by the billing process.

404. Explain use of "Retail for Merchandise Management" in a nutshell in SAP S/4HANA?

The empowered consumer has fundamentally changed retail. Companies need to establish a digital foundation to simplify their business with a detailed understanding of their customers' needs and the capabilities that allow them to serve customers individually and seamlessly.

Companies need to respond to the increasing need to engage customers at the right moment, consistently, and across multiple sales channels and technologies. A real-time retail platform helps companies transform their business and makes new business models possible, which can in turn increase revenue, profitability, and market share. SAP S/4HANA as a digital core helps companies to achieve these business goals.

405. Explain use of "Store Layout Management" in a nutshell in SAP S/4HANA?

Companies strive to offer products in the right place and at the right time in order to meet consumer needs and expectations. Through well-designed store layouts, retailers aim to create a convenient and appealing shopping experience, which is further enhanced by the optimum presentation of the merchandise on shelves, racks, and other in-store display fixtures, taking into account the number of products on display. This can be executed using a third-party space management solution.

406. Explain use of "Retail Price Management" in a nutshell in SAP S/4HANA?

A key aspect of how retailers address the market is the price strategy. That is, sales prices are planned based on various factors such as purchasing prices and margin goals, taking into consideration what consumers are willing to pay for products in stores or through non-store channels. Once a price strategy has been defined, it needs to be implemented, for example, by making the relevant sales prices available to stores and all other sales channels.

407. Explain use of "Pre-configured Master Tenant" in SAP S/4HANA Best Practices in a nutshell?

Pre-configured master tenant is a ready-to-run customer application with all the best practice content already configured. This ready to run application is usually activated for the customer during the PREPARE phase and used during the EXPLORE phase to demonstrate the starting point of configurations.

408. Explain use of "Configuration Guides" in SAP S/4HANA Best Practices in a nutshell?

These are easy-to-use, step-by-step configuration guides for those customers that want to manually configure the system. One use case is for those customers already on SAP SuccessFactors that want to add additional modules and may want to manually configure the new module.

409. Explain use of "Configuration Workbook" in SAP S/4HANA Best Practices in a nutshell?

Configuration workbook is a documentation of all the settings within the SAP Best Practices shown within Microsoft Excel spreadsheets. Customers can easily use these spreadsheets to confirm the settings and add additional customer specific settings. This is usually completed during the EXPLORE phase.

410. Explain use of "Demonstration Scripts" in SAP S/4HANA Best Practices in a nutshell?

Demonstration scripts and demonstration tenants can be used during the EXPLORE Phase to identify additional configuration that is needed beyond the Best Practices content.

411. Explain use of "Sample Test Data in SAP S/4HANA Best Practices" in a nutshell?

Sample test data and process steps are provided so that testing by SAP and/or the customer can be accelerated. It contains pre-built trackers for capturing testing results.

412. Explain use of "Process Diagrams in SAP S/4HANA Best Practices" in a nutshell?

Many customers want to document their HR processes. SAP Best Practices already contain the processes in process diagrams. These diagrams can be compared to customer requirements or used as a starting point for the final process flows for the customer solution.

413. Explain use of "Sample HR Forms in SAP S/4HANA SAP SuccessFactors Best Practices" in a nutshell?

Sample HR Forms are provided so that the testing process can be accelerated. Many SAP SuccessFactors modules use forms built in XML format. SAP Best Practices already have many examples of forms in xml format that customers can use as-is or modify for their unique requirements.

414. Explain "SAP SuccessFactors implementation projects iterations" in a nutshell?

Usually in SAP SuccessFactors implementation projects there are three or fewer iterations.

Agile Build: Iterative Iterations with Incremental Configurations

Sprint 1: During Iteration 1, best practice content is usually activated

Sprint 2: During iteration 2, the highest priority configurations and all changes from the best practice content are completed

Sprint 3: During Iteration 3, any changes discovered during Iteration 2 walkthrough are corrected and all remaining configurations are completed

At the end of the last iteration, all the configuration settings have been set, the migration scripts have been completed, and the interfaces have been set up.

NOTES

NOTES

NOTES

NOTES

NOTES

CHAPTER 7

SAP S/4 HANA and SAP Activate – Test Your Knowledge

1. What are the main advantages and benefits of using SAP Best practices?

2. Which elements are included in the guided configuration?

3. Describe the key elements and changes in the SAP Activate framework?

4. Which elements of SAP Activate do you expect your team will benefits from the most?

5. Name the 6 key characteristics of SAP Activate? Which ones are in particular important in your project context?

6. Why is the setup of project governance particularly important in an Agile context?

7. Which methodologies are succeeded by SAP Activate?

NOTES

NOTES

NOTES

NOTES

NOTES

NOTES

NOTES

CHAPTER 8

SAP S/4 HANA and SAP Activate – Key Takeaways

SAP Activate is the combination of SAP Best practices, tools for an assisted implementation and agile methodology to simplify the adoption of SAP S/4 HANA.

SAP Activate delivers ready-to-run business processes optimized for SAP S/4 HANA with a reference solution.

SAP Activate provides best practices for migration, integration and configuration for SAP S/4 HANA.

SAP Activate supports different starting points for customers to adopt SAP S/4 HANA - new implementation, system conversion and landscape transformation.

SAP Activate accelerates the initial implementation of SAP S/4 HANA and is designed for continuous innovation.

SAP Activate methodology is applicable outside of the SAP S/4HANA space with other SAP products in the cloud and on-premise.

SAP Best Practices also cover integration and migration fundamentals. They are designed to guide you through an optimal migration process, whether you are moving from a legacy SAP system or a non-SAP database. Business processes from SAP Best Practices when activated or scoped give you a reference solution with sample data included in the product, clear guidelines, and step-by-step directions on how to move from your current landscape to your goal.

SAP Activate starts with SAP Best Practices for any implementation, and uses a single methodology for all deployment modes - cloud, hybrid, on-premise. The goal of SAP Activate is to help customers take advantage of all the power and potential of SAP S/4HANA, tailored to their circumstances and business needs.

Example of New Implementation

New or existing SAP customers implementing a new SAP S/4 HANA system with initial data load.

Currently the majority of our customers are choosing the new implementation when they transition to SAP S4/HANA. This includes existing customers that use this scenario to re-think their processes and to take advantage of the simplified solution that SAP S/4HANA represents.

The next scenario in terms of popularity is the system conversion.

Example of System Conversion

System conversion - Complete conversion of an existing SAP Business Suite system to SAP S/4 HANA.

In the system conversion case, the project teams are doing a series of migration and conversion activities as they go through the steps of moving the system from ECC6 on any DB to ECC6 on SAP HANA and then moving it into the SAP S/4HANA code base. All these activities are done through the SAP upgrade manager.

Example of Landscape Transformation

Consolidation of current regional SAP Business Suite landscape into one global SAP S/4HANA system.

It includes the consolidation of multiple systems into one system or carving out one company code to SAP S/4HANA.

SAP Activate methodology consists of one simple, modular and agile methodology and is the successor of ASAP and SAP Launch methodologies. It supports all S/4 HANA transition scenarios.

SAP Activate methodology provides full support for initial deployment and continuous business innovation.

SAP Activate methodology provides harmonized implementation approach for cloud, on-premise and hybrid deployments.

This methodology provides broad coverage of SAP Solutions starting with SAP S/4 HANA and enables co-innovation with customers and is accessible for partners.

SAP Activate methodology is designed to support a broad coverage of SAP solutions including, but not limited to, SAP S/4HANA, SAP Business

Suite on-premise, SAP SuccessFactors, and SAP Ariba.

The methodology has a harmonized structure and approach with multiple flavors (or roadmaps) that support delivery of specific type of project. The new implementation scenario covers not only SAP S/4HANA, but also implementation of other SAP products and solutions, such as SAP Business Suite, SAP Ariba, SAP SuccessFactors and others.

SAP Activate succeeds ASAP 8 methodology and SAP Launch methodology.

The SAP Activate methodology content can be accessed on the SAP Jam site and the detailed SAP Activate roadmaps in the Roadmap Viewer tool. These environments are updated on regular basis and provide always the up-to-date information for users of SAP Activate methodology.

The Jam site environment provides a great place to learn about the SAP Activate methodology and to discuss the approach with experts.

The Roadmap Viewer, on the other hand, provides detailed roadmaps for specific project types with granular details including solution specific accelerators and the product guidance needed by the project teams. Project teams transitioning to SAP S/4HANA or implementing other SAP solutions should use the detailed guidance in the Roadmap Viewer.

URLs

URL to access Roadmap Viewer tool

http://bit.ly/SAPRoadmapViewer

URL to access SAP Jam site

http://bit.ly/SAPActivate

For the new implementation scenario, the SAP Activate pillars of Best Practices and Methodology are fully available; the new Guided Configuration tools are available for the new cloud implementations. For new on-premise, or private cloud implementations, the configuration is done with the Implementation Guide (IMG) in the SAP S/4HANA system, for example, the SPRO transaction or via SAP Solution Manager.

In the System Conversion scenario, the project teams can take advantage of the methodology, best practices for migration, and integration. However, the Guided Configuration tools will not be used because the project team is converting existing configuration from source system to the target system. As a result, there is no need to use the guided configuration tools. The project team will use the IMG to configure the system or to adjust the configuration settings.

The Landscape Transformation is a scenario in which the team needs to make decisions about what Best Practices will be applicable in the project depending on the type of the solution that is being implemented. For scenarios where a customer relies on SAP Best Practices, the team can use the pre-delivered content (for example, the scope items). For scenarios where a customer will reuse their existing processes, the team will not use the Best Practices content. Methodology is again fully applicable in this scenario and the Guided Configuration will be used only for cloud solutions that the customer deploys (in on-premise solutions the consultants will use the IMG to configure the solution).

If you have not already done so, we recommend that you use the link https://bit.ly/SAPActivate to request access to the SAP Activate methodology Jam site. You can use the site to learn more about the methodology and to engage with the methodology experts in SAP and in the SAP partner ecosystem.

References

SAP Activate on sap.com :   http://sap.com/activate

SAP Service Marketplace : http://service.sap.com/solutionpackages

SAP S/4 HANA Trail Page : http://www.sap.com/s4hana-trial

SAP Best Practices Explorer : http://rapid.sap.com/bp

SAP Roadmap Viewer : https://go.sap.corp/roadmapviewer

SAP Activate Cook-book : https://go.sap.corp/cookbook

Hybrid Integration Page : http://service.sap.com/hybrid

SAP Solution Manager 7.2 - References

General overview - http://support.sap.com/solutionmanager

Focused solutions overview - http://support.sap.com/focused

Documentation - http://help.sap.com/solutionmanager72

Learning Maps and Guided Discovery Tutorials - http://support.sap.com/ekt-solutionmanager

SAP Community Network (SCN) - https://wiki.scn.sap.com/wiki/display/

SM/Getting+Started+WIKI+for+SAP+Solution+Manager

SCN Discussions - https://scn.sap.com/community/it-management/alm/solution-manager

Technical Info - https://apps.support.sap.com/sap/support/pam?hash=pvnr%3D01200615320900006067%26pt%3Dg%257Cd

SAP delivers a set of ready-to-run best practice processes with SAP S/4HANA. SAP Best Practices provide the foundation for each implementation and give customers a jump start and reference solution from which to begin the implementation project. In addition to these core, foundation SAP Best Practices, SAP delivers set of integration and migration best practices.

We can increase value proposition and time-to-value with SAP Best practices.

SAP delivers a set of ready-to-run best practice processes with SAP S/4HANA.

SAP Best Practices provide the foundation for each implementation and give customers a jump start and reference solution from which to begin the implementation project.

In addition to these core, foundation SAP Best Practices, SAP delivers set of integration and migration best practices

The project team can set up their sandbox environment quickly using the Cloud Appliance Library.

Solution Validation Workshop

A Solution Validation workshop is not intended to educate participants. We recommend project teams to plan project team enablement and walkthroughs prior to these workshops to keep the workshop focus on the fit and gaps.

In these workshops the consultants will start with the overall solution before drilling down to process and function detail. Consultants will use the Best Practices documentation including the Business Process models to help facilitate the workshops.

The objective for the workshop is to challenge changes to standard functionality and determine if there is a need for changes or enhancements. Any changes need to be tied to business value or benefits.

The output of the solution validation workshop is a list of delta requirements and gaps.

Delta Solution Design Workshop

During this workshop, the team creates a design for addressing the delta requirements and resolving the gaps.

Customer business users have a key role in contributing during the design and acceptance of delta solution design.

Project team uses SAP Solution Manager as a toolset for solution documentation, including the delta design documents.

The methodology recommends the use of 'Road Shows' to gain business acceptance, especially in larger projects.

Purpose of Fit/Gap Analysis

- The Fit/Gap Analysis has the following main objectives:
- The primary objective is to have an updated and approved Scope Baseline to move into the Realization phase
- Validate pre-activated or pre-assembled solution in the Sandbox system
- Drive towards adopting SAP standard processes
- Ensure that SAP implementation meets customer's business needs
- Discover, clarify, and negotiate solution design
- Identify and capture delta business requirements and gaps (on top of the initial Sandbox system)
- Prioritize delta requirements and gaps
- Minimize the need for rework during Realization.

Made in the USA
San Bernardino, CA
13 November 2019